VILLA DETAILS

OVIDIO GUAITA

VILLA DETAILS

INTRODUCTION BY
NANI PRINA

CARTAGO

AKNOWLEDGEMENTS

This book is the outcome of the author's collaboration with "VilleGiardini" Magazine and research at the Department of History and Restoration, Faculty of Architecture, University of Florence.
A portion of the historical research and a number of drawings were undertaken by students attending the Sculpted Architecture seminar given by the author in the academic year 1995-96, as part of the course in History of Art under Fauzia Farneti.

Special thanks are therefore due to my students:
Silvia Campanella, Paolo Carlo Capozzi, Michela Carli, Paola Cesarini, Anna Maria Giulia Costa, Daria Cresti, Lisa Dell'Omarino, Sara Fabbri, Alessandro Formiglia, Gerardo Giacchetti, Elisa Innocenti, Francesca Latini, Alessandra Lazzeri, Vania Lovat, Cinzia Lucciarini De Vincenzi,

Alessandro Marioni, Sara Marrani, Monica Milani, Annalisa Morelli, Mariangela Murgo, Doriana Nenna, Concetta Pacifico, Bianca Pelligra, Giuseppe Pezzano, Clara Piccioli, Angelamaria Quartulli, Nausicaa Rahmati, Claudia Rangoni, Nicola Ripanti, Desirée Roso, Paola Scaringella, Valeria Sgarbossa, Grazia Strati, Elisa Tommasini, Fabiana Toni.

Photographs by
Ovidio Guaita

Art Director
Giorgio Seppi

Graphic Design and
Editorial Production
Studio Priori, Milan
and Silvia Rossi

Translated by
Peter Eustace

Edited by
Caroline Harcourt

Published in the United Kingdom by CARTAGO, an imprint of KEA Publishing Services Ltd., 63 Edith Grove, London SW10 0LB.
©2000

info@cartago.net - www.cartago.net

ISBN 1-900826-28-3

Original title: Segni di Villa
© 1998 Arnoldo Mondadori Editore S.p.A., Milan.

Printed by Artes Gráficas Toledo, Spain.
D.L. TO: 1271 - 2000

Pages 2 & 3, from the left: Chinese window (Suzhov), shutters at Jaipur (Hawa Mahal) and a tympanun in Caracas (Venezuela).
Pages 4 & 5, from the left: mosaic in Madeira, baluster at Antisrabe (Madagascar), the facade of Os Dobris, detail of a door in Nikko, Japan, and the clock at Montalto in Puglia, Italy.
Pages 6 & 7, from the left: rainwater spouts, a door in Peru (Trujillo) and detail of a facade in Peru (Trujillo).
Page 8: window at Maracaibo (Venezuela).

CONTENTS

FOREWORD

In the course of his long and productive collaboration with "VilleGiardini" Magazine, I suggested to Ovidio Guaita that he should compile an archive of details – that is, photograph architectural elements which, through function, form and aesthetic effect, exemplify and emphasise specific features of the world of villas, since credentials and ownership are often expressed precisely through such details. This was the starting-point for a huge and unusual repertory of architectural elements, which represents both an intriguing document of human creativity and a useful consultation and reference work for "experts" in the field. Windows, doors, staircases, tympanums and arches, spires and pinnacles, balusters and parapets, guttering, drain-pipes and spouts, shields, masks and

sundials, as both decorative and functional elements, here stimulate the curiosity of admirers of all that is fine and beautiful. The book is an astonishing anthology of photographs in which, for the most part, drawings, historical remarks and contemporary technical information stimulate the thoughts of professional designers by suggesting appropriate solutions for effective creation or renovation of this prestigious architectural heritage: the villa.

Nani Prina

Publisher of "VilleGiardini"

Left:
Medicean Villa, Poggio a Caiano,
Florence.

VILLA DETAILS

This book illustrates two thousand years of the villa, displaying distinctive hallmarks, architectural details and the most original, fascinating and bizarre decorations from residences all over the world. It is an historic and geographical itinerary embracing everything that "makes a villa", from the country mansions of Imperial Rome to contemporary, post-modern and minimalist homes, from California to Taiwan, from Iceland to South Africa, moving among hugely different peoples, cultures, traditions, materials and climates. The Latin term "*villa*" at the time of Imperial Rome was used for both country hamlets and patrician residences, whether farms or out-of-town homes. Its counterpart was the "*domus*", a town-home for single-family units, comparable to modern day apartments. In the fourteen-hundreds, the term villa was embraced by the Italian language, especially in its aristocratic sense, while the farming-residential function incorporated in the Latin use of the word was extended with the addition of formal and courtly connotations which gave definitive identification to the new kind of country building. The villa is rightly considered as a largely "Italian" phenomenon, and it is no coincidence that there is no equivalent term in other languages, which either utilise the term "villa" itself or else words more closely related to castles, palaces or farmhouses. But what exactly is a modern villa? First and foremost, it is a single-family residence – in a suburban or countryside setting – distinguished by cultured or artistically praiseworthy design which blends harmoniously with surrounding Nature, relating to its setting through green areas such as parks or gardens. Yet the most characteristic and noble aspect is the inclusion of various "distinguishing hallmarks" such as heraldic shields, storey dividers, bands, architectural orders, statues and busts, stucco-work and the like. The Italian Renaissance model was assimilated, albeit much later, throughout Europe. Designers in Middle-Europe and Britain wholeheartedly embraced the style and

Above: El Castillo, a ranchhouse in the Argentine pampas.
Centre: one of the most important historical villas in Florida, at Key West.

fashion, while adapting forms to local building traditions. The advent of the colonies further enriched the original designs with new and different details and accents related to local climate, construction materials, architecture and art. A kaleidoscope of forms, colours and applications characterised the villas of the new worlds, making them entirely different from those built in the owners' homelands. The echoes of fashion and trends in the mother-country reached these distant lands in diluted form, while customs and methods blended in out-of-focus recollections. In light of these considerations, and not without some degree of generalisation, it can be said that villas throughout the world are inspired by three main concepts: the European villa, the model most closely resembling the original Italian style; the "native" villas, initially built in the wake of European exploration (as in Mexico, India, China, Japan or Morocco); and the colonial villas, inspired by European styles yet greatly influenced by local settings and cultures. In other words, while the colonists spread this style in an attempt to reproduce a feeling of the mother country, they could not but take

Above: Reykjavik (Iceland): Government House.
Right: the ancient residence of Moritzburg, Germany, currently a museum.

into account the settings where these villas were built, so much so that pure white Carrara marble was replaced by painted wood, and verandas were built instead of the Palladian "*pronaos*". The settlers were seeking a *modus vivendi* with the new worlds, be they in the West Indies, the East Indies or the Black Continent. This saw the emergence of Dutch Cape villas in South Africa, the *fazendas* of Rio de Janeiro, the far-flung, variously painted farm-villas of Iceland and the all-embracing palaces of Korea.

These residences emerged everywhere as the *topos* of life in the country, dedicated to intellectual idleness and salubrious rural life, as well as landmarks in the management of large estates. Shields, emblems and coats of arms decorated these residences and land-holdings of the gentry, indelibly reflecting the status of their owners. Such testimony of a courtly past today narrates the history of these villas, the changes in ownership, embellishing them to the point of representing – even today for the elite few – an elegant visiting card. As time passes and fashions come and go, ancient and modern implements mark their movements. Amidst tympanums and festoons, simple cornices and massive stucco-works, today, as in the past, timepieces characterize outlooks and, just like shields and busts, link villas to the great myths and mysteries of life. The "possession" of Time, especially in past centuries, meant control over the destiny of people. It is no coincidence that such instruments appear on facades, so that everyone can make use of them without entering or crossing the sacred threshold of the owner of the manor. Elegant screens protect such privacy, while equally becoming an occasion for embellishment. Yet the glory of every courtly celebration in any villa – in all latitudes – is the entrance, the true columns of Hercules in all such residences. These, as few other features, bear witness to the taste, culture and even the worries of the owner. Yet economic power, just like political power, has never been able to detach itself from religious hegemony. The presence of a place of worship within the villa

Above: the Baroque Summer Residence of the Royal Family at Queluz, not far from Lisbon

itself was not only a matter of considerable convenience but also a question of enormous prestige, while a similar chapel outside, open to the "work folk", consolidated the power of the gentry by ensuring control of even the divine aspects of everyday life. The intention of this book is to travel "round the world in thirty details", taking in the most evocative and curious examples spread over five continents. This is an itinerary which reveals innumerable interpretations of the villa and that ancient aspiration of mankind to create a congenial habitat reflecting his needs, styles, tastes and humours. It is an itinerary across vastly different ethnic and architectural realities, where land and climate have joined or separated, where the oceans have carved tiny archipelagos or huge continents, where endless microcosms have for millennia guarded techniques, traditions and beliefs. In the complex human and political geography of our planet, these "details", so different yet so similar, demonstrate how architecture is one of the few unifying and socialising arts of mankind. They also show how art is a *trait-d'union*, crossing borders, barriers and opposing ideals to help give a more universal meaning to this global village called Earth.

PLACES DOCUMENTED

NORTH AMERICA
1 Arizona
2 Bermuda
3 California
4 Canada
5 Florida
6 Hawaii
7 Louisiana
8 Mississippi
9 New Mexico
10 New York
11 Puerto Rico
12 Rhode Island
13 Tennessee
14 Virginia

23 Jamaica
24 Guatemala
25 Maranhao
26 Mexico
27 Peru
28 Trinidad and Tobago
29 Venezuela

EUROPE
30 Austria
31 Belgium
32 Cyprus
33 Vatican City
34 Denmark
35 France
36 Germany

47 Poland
48 Portugal
49 United Kingdom
50 Czech Republic
51 Russia
52 San Marino
53 Slovakia
54 Spain
55 Sweden
56 Switzerland
57 Hungary

AFRICA
58 Algeria
59 Madagascar
60 Morocco

69 Bahrein
70 China
71 South Corea
72 Dubai
73 Philippines
74 Japan
75 Hong Kong
76 India
77 Indonesia
78 Iran
79 Israel
80 Malaysia
81 Maldives
82 Oman
83 Pakistan
84 Palestine

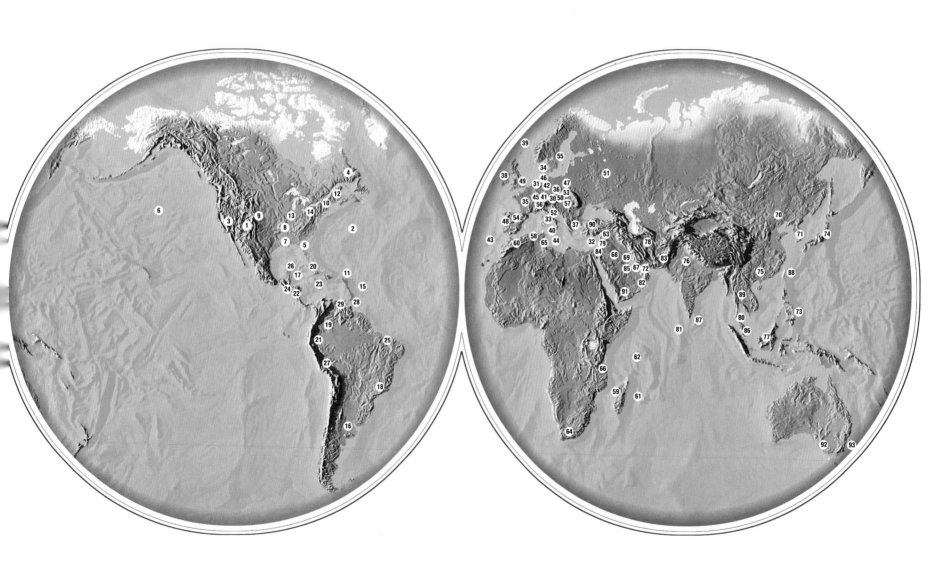

SOUTH AND CENTRAL AMERICA
15 Antigua
16 Argentina
17 Belize
18 Brazil
19 Colombia
20 Cuba
21 Ecuador
22 El Salvador

37 Greece
38 Ireland
39 Iceland
40 Italy
41 Liechtenstein
42 Luxembourg
43 Madeira
44 Malta
45 Monaco
46 Holland

61 Réunion
62 Seychelles
63 Syria
64 South Africa
65 Tunisia
66 Zanzibar

ASIA
67 Abu Dhabi
68 Saudi Arabia

85 Qatar
86 Singapore
87 Sri Lanka
88 Taiwan
89 Thailand
90 Turkey
91 Yemen

OCEANIA
92 Australia
93 New Zealand

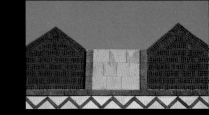

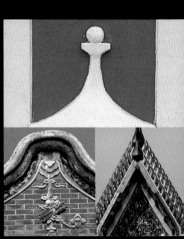

The Testimony of Classicism

Orders are one of the most typical hallmarks of Classicism. Columns resembling petrified tree-trunks or the human body, capitals like human heads, scrolls like female hair-plaits, grooves resembling drapery.

Classicism is thus a combination of aesthetic canons and an artistic style inspired by classic culture, worthy of standing as a model through the exemplary level of perfection achieved – as in Greek (especially between the V and IV centuries B.C.) and Roman architecture. It is no coincidence that it was the Roman architect Vetruvius who, in the I century B.C., took up the classic building tradition which later inspired the theoreticians of the Renaissance, themselves the mediators between tradition and innovation. This tradition saw the spread of frontons, elegant "stage-curtains" decorating the plain structures supporting roofs, tympanums and arches. Hermae, talamons and caryatids alternated with fretwork, arabesques and scrolls, supporting and embellishing pronaoi, frontons, storey-markers and cornices. The centre of the facade was further ornamented with festoons, having a merely decorative role, flanked by acroteria, obelisks, urns and vases, joined everywhere by towers reaching to the heavens (yet more probably intended to dominate the surrounding landscape). Domes, both true and false, externally imitate the globe and internally contain imitations of the celestial skyscape. Yet other details were by no means overlooked: even plain and functional guttering is embellished with cymatia, "little waves" in painted terracotta, and rainwater spouts are disguised behind gargoyles.

The ultimate hallmark, the final testimony of Classicism, is the garret. In fact, far from being a classical element, it exemplified the transition between Classicism and its humanist renaissance. With its defensive functions, it is a reminder of the barbarian invasions that destroyed the Empire, as well as of the castle keeps and the Middle Ages, the dark age which nevertheless carried the West towards the Renaissance.

Classicism came to life again in Humanism. It was present as a set of rules but equally as a sublime source of inspiration, where Man was at last at the centre of the Universe.

Pronaoi

From the Greek Prónáos (pró, "in front" and naos "*cell*"), originally used to indicate the porticoed chamber placed in front of the cell of classic temples. It was therefore exclusively associated with religious architecture and it was only with Roman architecture that it entered the public sphere, thus giving monumental status even to ordinary civic buildings. It was extensively used in Imperial Rome, but it was with the rediscovery of the classic world, initially with Humanism and later in the Renaissance, that the pronaos took on a decisive role in the composition of the facades of villas. Initially, orders were incorporated into the facade itself. Alberti effectively designed a practical treatise in the Palazzo Rucellai, Florence, where all three orders are represented and catalogued. Yet the pronaos was soon detached from the facade as such to acquire its own spatial dimension, as in classical examples.

It was an architectural and thus human element, scientifically proportioned through the use of modules and complex proportional parameters. In the Doric order, the diameter of a column at the base is one-fifth of its height, reflecting the same ratio as that between the foot and the height of a male athlete. In the Ionic order, on the other hand, the ratio was one-eighth, since reference was made to the proportions of the female body, just as the volutes of the capital recall women's hair plaits and the grooves in the drum resemble the folds of rich fabrics. These modules were therefore used in buildings to reflect the same proportional ratios found in the human body. Buildings thus reflected Nature, in which the human body was considered to be the highest expression.

In 1570, Andrea Palladio published his *Four Books of Architecture*, the treatise in which he translated his ideas about buildings, villas and temples into drawings. In this work, Palladio referred to previous treatises by Vignola and Serlio, who provided the starting-point for a review of the classic tradition, itself rediscovered and renewed. He preferred rich orders for lordly villas and palaces, while the Tuscan order was considered most suitable for farmhouses. Special emphasis was given to the spacing between the columns, the dimensions of which were closely related to those of the orders themselves. It was thanks to this attention to detail that the pronaos acquired increasing importance and grandiosity in the facades of Italian Renaissance villas and – mediated by the designs of the great Vicenza-born architect – they were to become

A classic Ionic pronaos in the reconstruction by a Renaissance theoretician. From the Humanist period onwards, the pronaos was increasingly incorporated into aristocratic mansions.

On the tropical island of Praslin, in the Seychelles archipelago, French architecture is filtered through local traditions. Stone is replaced by wood, the columns are slimmer and the pronaos itself is much lighter than in the Old Continent.

One of the secondary entrances to the City Palace, Jaipur, known as "the pink city" after the costly sandstone used in the construction of most of its buildings.

The large, Neo-Classic pronaos of the eighteen-hundreds overlooks the main square of Spanish Town, the small settlement founded by the Spanish in 1523 which was the capital of Jamaica until the middle of last century.

Metopes and triglyphs in this frieze surmounting a Renaissance pronaos. The metopes have bucranes, recalling the animal sacrifices of the Hellenist period.

This elegant pronaos in Jerusalem is completely unlike classical tradition; its three small domes interrelate with the much larger main dome of the building.

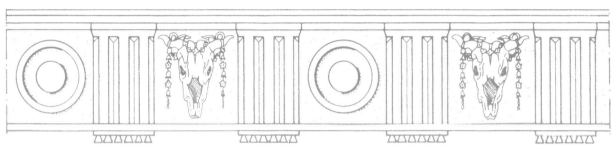

a recurrent element in courtly residential architecture.

All skilled designers develop personal rules for determining the proportions between the pronaos and the main body of the building: some, like Raphael and Peruzzi, emphasise axes, others the height of the front section and others still the tympanum crowning the facade and hiding the two slopes of the roof. Equally, some architects prefer the "gigantic" orders, introduced by Alberti but redeveloped in great detail by Michelangelo, who subordinated frameworks, dimensions and the spacing between columns to the compositional axes of the facade. When dimensions are not enlarged, the orders are overlapped to form double pronaoi: the one on the ground floor has the main entrance, while the one on the first floor has a balcony.

In the sixteen-hundreds, Inigo Jones took up Palladio's experience and introduced classicism to England. His mansions were for some considerable time important landmarks for contemporary architects: the large pasturelands of Yorkshire and Devon welcomed ethereal pronaoi, often built using pure white Italian marble. The Humanist "loggia", inspired by Mediaeval cloisters, became a vague memory, a timid aperture towards the external world, the last vestige of a political climate too tense to keep pace with changing times. The pronaos was even "exported" to the colonies where, although almost always in wood, it bore ideal testimony to classicism, as well as being an element ensuring immediate and clear formal qualification to the homes of colonists and adventurers.

Three different ways in which the pronaos is used to characterise a villa. Below: Palladio's "Rotonda" near Vicenza, one of the finest villas the fifteen-hundreds architect designed but also, in absolute terms, one of the most interesting in that it represents a detailed interpretation of classicism.

Far left: the entrance to the Sultan's Palace, Yogyyakarta, on the island of Java, Indonesia, where European and local architecture interact harmoniously. Left: a villa on the outskirts of Colombo, Sri Lanka, an interesting interpretation of Anglo-Saxon influences.

Even in different periods and places, the pronaos maintains certain common elements. From top to bottom: Villa Pisani, Vicenza (XVII century), a more modest eighteen-hundreds mansion in San Diego and a regal main entrance to a contemporary villa in Honolulu. Side: the imposing pronaos of Villa Maldura, Monselice (near Padua), raised to the level of the main floor and accessed by two opposing staircases.

Orders

Mankind has always attempted to develop theories to explain the presiding relationships of the Universe. It was around these laws that theoreticians developed their formulas which sought an architectural order underlying harmonious proportions which would also express "goodness"; an idea of interior beauty which may attain intellectual or spiritual, as well as aesthetic, formal order.

An order is therefore a defined and stable system or set of rules through which columns, capitals, trabeations and frontons are reciprocally harmonised, as classified in ancient Greece. Capitals having forms similar to the Doric order had already appeared in Cretian and Minoan architecture, together with the idea of supporting a load on a large "cushion" on top of an upright element. Volutes and floral decorations, the forerunners of the Ionic capital, were, on the other hand, common in the ancient architecture of the East, while grooved trabeations and mouldings appeared in Egypt. Yet it was thanks to the fervid cultural climate created by Greek civilisation that these individual elements were classified in a systematic manner and developed into a set of rules capable of giving life to well-proportioned and harmonious buildings.

The two fundamental orders – the Doric and the Ionic – took shape between the VI and the VII century A.D. as representations of two different races and cultures within a single Hellenic civilisation. They emerged in different historical contexts: continental Greece invaded by the Dorians and Asian-island Greece occupied by the Ionians. In the Doric order, in particular, the basic elements were developed from the wooden buildings erected by Greek progenitors. Triglyphs seem to recall the beam heads of chains, while metopes resemble the original axes or clay slabs separating the area beneath the roof. In the Ionic order, the dentils of the trabeation derive from the projecting heads of the small beams that held up the wooden floors on which the roofing was supported. Columns themselves were indicated as "petrified" ancient tree trunks which once made up the vertical supports of early monumental buildings. Also, just like tree-trunks, columns were wider at the base than at the top and they were grooved to resemble the vertical markings in the bark. Yet columns may also be seen as the

Above: capitals are widely used in Islamic architecture, although decorative motifs are very different.

Following page: an amazing capital at the Maharajah's Palace, Indore, northern India. Elements of classic and native architecture are skilfully blended in this extremely evocative work.

6

8

7

9

25

26

27

1

4

1. *Corinthian capital.*
2. *Tel Aviv, Israel.*
3. *Nicosia, Cyprus.*
4. *Marrakech, Morocco.*
5. *Damascus, Siria.*
6. *Singapore.*
7. *Taegu, South Corea.*
8. *Cusco, Peru.*
9. *Singapore.*
10. *New Delhi, India.*
11. *Jerusalem, Israel.*
12. *Singapore.*
13. *Prambanan, Indonesia.*
14. *Kyongju, South Corea.*
15. *Shangai, China.*
16. *Macao.*
17. *Los Angeles, California.*
18. *Cusco, Peru.*
19. *Palm Beach, Florida.*
20. *Palermo, Italy.*
21. *Macao.*
22. *Los Angeles, California.*
23. *Indore, India.*
24. *Anuradhapura, Sri Lanka.*
25. *Ayuttaya, Thailand.*
26. *Merida, Mexico.*
27. *Bangkok, Thailand.*
28. *Zanzibar, Tanzania.*
29. *Quito, Ecuador.*
30. *Seoul, South Corea.*
31. *Lima, Peru.*
32. *Yogyakarta, Indonesia.*
33. *Taipei, Taiwan.*
34. *Antananarivo, Madagascar.*
35. *Ayuttaya, Thailand.*
36. *Miami Beach, Florida.*

2

3

5

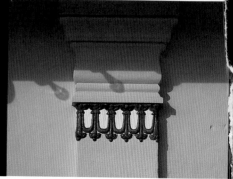

21

22

23

24

17

20

18

19

33

34

35

10

12

15

1

13

14

16

29

30

31

32

transposition of the human body into architecture. The ancient Greeks modulated their buildings in accordance with the proportions existing between various parts of the body. The Parthenon, Athens, is perhaps the most mature example of the Doric order, whereas the Erectheum has the same status for the Ionic. The Corinthian order emerged as an evolution of the Ionic, retaining all the basic elements with the exception of the capital. Pliny attributed its invention to the Athenian sculptor Callimachus, a pupil of Phydias, who was struck by the sight, surmounting the tomb of a young girl in Corinth, of a basket of votary offerings encircled by the leaves of an acanthus plant.

The classic orders of Greek origin were later joined by styles developed in Italy under the Romans. The composite order, first and foremost, created by including Ionic volutes in Corinthian capitals, was already in use at the time of Emperor Augustus and widely employed following the rediscovery of classic architecture from the Renaissance onwards. There was also the Tuscan order, derived from the Doric, and characterised by somewhat squatter forms. The invention of the order in ancient Greece was skilfully elaborated later by the Romans, who associated it with the use of arches; orders were catalogued and given a scientific basis in the Renaissance, when they were standardised in a rational structuring of architecture, especially by architects such as Filippo Brunelleschi and Leon Battista Alberti. Since then, gigantic, overlapping and rustic orders – as well as all kinds of other imaginative orders in the humanist and mannerist tradition – have spread throughout Europe and all over the world. The most recent period of rigorous application of orders was during Neo-Classicism. The original functions were often distorted, materials completely re-invented and the static functions of the various elements invalidated. Over the centuries and further away from Greece, orders have become decorative elements intended to emphasise the monumental nature of a building – often without performing any static functions whatsoever.

Frontons

Frontons are one of the elements that are shared by both East and West. They exist, admittedly in very modified forms, all over the world. Above: a fronton at Nikko, Japan. Below: a much more highly decorated and elaborate fronton crowning a villa in the historic centre of Bangkok. The gilt and painted wood characteristic of all South-East Asia is particularly evident.

Classic frontons usually have a shallow slope. The first Greek temples had flat, mud and straw roofs but, from the VIII century B.C., the invention of large, clay roofing tiles made it much easier to erect buildings with a rectangular ground plan – covered by roofs with two slopes – which also permitted installations at sharper angles. The fronton was richly decorated. The triangular space inside often contained bas-reliefs, while the summit and external angles of the fronton supported sculptures. Various theoreticians proposed personalised rules for the dimensions of this element, universally recognised as immensely elegant. Vitruvius himself suggested dividing the maximum length by nine to calculate the height between the top of the slope and the base. Designers in every country have studied such rules, subsequently developing their own original inventions independently of classical

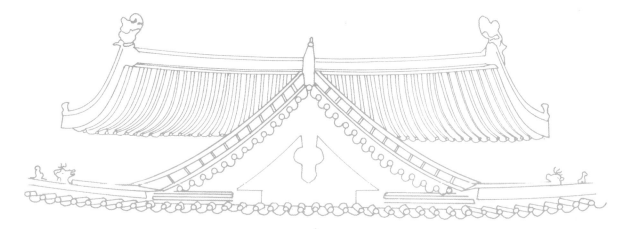

The swastika proudly placed in the centre of this fronton in Taegu, South Korea, should not be misinterpreted. Before it was imported into Europe, this motif was widely used in the East as a symbol of prosperity.

The complex roof of the Longxing Si Palace, built in southern China around 1052. The fronton is placed on one of the lesser sides of the residence

Residential "castles" were built in Denmark from the Middle Ages until last century. Considerable attention was always placed on decoration, at times with great informality, as in the case of this curved fronton where windows open between bas-reliefs.

Villa Parravicini, Como, Italy, set off by an elegant Neo-Classic fronton surmounted by three statues imitating the acroteria of ancient temples.

A broad fronton, characterised by emphatic dentils, dominates the facade of Templeton House, Long Island, New York.

dispositions. In Rome, many elements of the fronton were developed from the Hellenic tradition. These elements encompassed: the inclusion of figures in the tympanum, even in buildings characterised by the Ionic and Corinthian orders, these figures were sometimes in clay but, more frequently, in bronze (high-relief rather than full-round); a great many acroterial statues; and overlapping small bronze palms on the cymatium. However, unlike the Greek fronton, the Roman style is more acute: the cornices of the ramps are the same as those of the trabeation and vertical elements remain vertical rather than at right-angles to the line of the watershed. At the end of the I century B.C., the use of volcanic sand mixed with lime revolutionised building construction and transformed classic architecture. In Imperial Rome and, later, in Renaissance buildings, the fronton was gradually separated from the sloping roof to become an architectural element in its own right.

With the fall of the Roman Empire, a refined Byzantine interpretation of Classicism came to the fore where geometry held sway over details and decorations. The barbarian dark ages did not destroy the Imperial heritage as such, since the artistic tradition had already disappeared. From the Gothic period, the front part of the building was considered as a decorative rather than a functional element; the fronton was distinguished by vertical development and an acute arch or mullioned tympanum. With the late-Gothic, attention returned to the artistic heritage of Rome and, initially in the

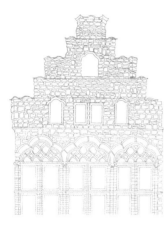

A stepped fronton, typical of northern Europe, crowning a mansion built in the 1200s at Malines, Belgium.

In this mansion in Cape Town, the two facades – one overlooking the road, the other facing the garden – are distinguished by two ethereal frontons emphasised by large volutes

A Japanese fronton where painted wood is joined by "terracotta" and a number of metal elements. Concave and convex curves give rise to unusual fluidity.

On the outskirts of Kandy, Sri Lanka, on the road to Colombo, this 1800s colonial mansion boasts a fronton with a highly personalised style.

The motif based on three statues crowning the summit and base corners, copied from Hellenic frontons, is a frequent design element. This particular fronton surmounts the Villa Rubini, built in the 1700s near Vicenza, Italy.

Renaissance and later in the Baroque period, frontons achieved exquisite formal elaboration and increasingly creativity, with curved, broken, scrolled and decorated forms with plaques, emblems, figures and mouldings.

In the mid-1500s, Venetian architect Andrea Palladio applied the fronton to villas, both in town and country settings, sure of interpreting the taste of the Italians who adored giving equal dignity to temples and aristocratic homes. His villa designs include a broad portico surmounted by a fronton, which was gradually also separated from the columns, which may or may not support it, in alternation with pillars and solid masonry. When columns were retained, column spacing – once measured in multiples of the diameter of the drum – was freed from classic rules and new proportions were experimented with.

In the XVIII century, with the advent of Neo-Classicism, a new way of thinking emerged and people sought release from the weight of their cultural history to re-discover purity in the simplicity of primitive origins. In their search for fundamental truths, philosophers observed the life and character of natural man, free from social conventions. The study of history for its own sake and the emergence of archaeology encouraged artists and architects to seek inspiration in a carefully reconstructed past. Hellenic frontons were rigidly imitated in Neo-Classic architecture, the last period in which this element was widely used. They disappeared with the arrival and generalised use of flat roofs in modern and contemporary architecture.

The fronton of the Lin An-Tai mansion in Taipei fully reveals its function of buffering the trussed roof. A large cornice acts as a moulding while, in the centre on top of exposed brickwork, there is a multi-coloured ceramic decoration.

Akureyri, northern Iceland: for six months' a year the sun rises for only a few hours a day. Light is fundamentally important, so that even the fronton is utilised to illuminate the interior, transforming it into a kind of huge roof terrace.

Tympanums and arches

The entrance to the 1700s Villa Loschi Zilieri Dal Verme at Monteviale, the Veneto, Italy, is an arch surmounted by a sinuous tympanum interrupted to include the coat of arms of the owner.

A similar design approach, albeit more imaginative and highly decorative, is used in this window in the Ajakbash Palace, Aleppo, Syria.

Doors and windows have always had an upper enclosure, however simple, even if merely an architrave or jamb. Yet crossing a threshold has always had a religious meaning and primitive decorations of doorways are apotropaic elements associated with pagan culture, such as small busts placed as guardians of the home or tiles bearing six-pointed stars for good luck. A combination of symbols which, with their magical meanings, were intended to keep away or ward off evil spirits. With the advent of Christianity, these elements were replaced by religious symbols, such as the monogram of Christ, IHS inscribed in a circle.

The formal definition of building rules in the Hellenic and Roman period saw the development of tympanums (triangular or curved) as decorations placed above the architrave. They were simple enclosures that had no load-bearing functions and were decorated with paintings or bas-reliefs. They were not necessarily triangular in shape. Indeed, the upper part may be curved and, in this instance, they are said to be "cambered". The curves are generally shallow, but there are examples of round-arch designs. In some installations, triangular and curved tympanums alternate with each other and the roofing slopes may be terminated at the base and summit with scrolls and volutes. These variants, however, are almost always attributable to the Baroque period.

In the boldest examples, the architrave "dissolves", giving rise to an arch which may be round, pointed or mixed in outline, such as those inspired by Islamic art. The Romans adopted jambed doors, which were used particularly in private architecture. After the IV century, architectural frames moved away from classic orders, so much so that from the paleo-Christian age to the High Middle Ages, door and window frames were defined at most by a cornice. In some cases, Roman archaeological finds were re-utilised. Classic outlines returned with Federician architecture, flanked by parastas and crowned by trabeations and triangular frontons.

In France, the concentric arch doorway achieved a formal style, which was widely utilised in the Gothic period.

The latter age saw a radical transformation of the Romanesque doorway: the arches became

Style in Cuba is by no means only the colonial Baroque of the Spanish. The Cubans have always been able to recreate outside influences, as in this distinctly eclectic 1800s tympanum in Havana.

The colonial Trujillo exhibits all the architectural tradition of Peru. Baroque and Neo-Classic blend to create evocative courtly forms found in few other places in Latin America.

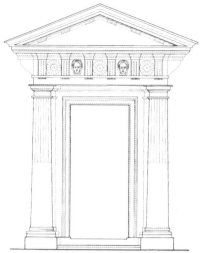

pointed and the external order was surmounted by a triangular, cusped fronton, often flanked by two spires.

In the late-Gothic period in Catalonia, the so-called "Durazzesque" doorway became common, where the low arch was framed by a face outlined by more or less elaborate moulding. Aedicule-style doors and windows later became extremely popular, with a jambed or ordered chamber, framed by columns or parastas supporting a triangular or semi-circular tympanum.

In the XV century, decorative elements surmounting doors appeared all over Europe, depicting religious scenes such as the *Annunciation*, the *Adoration of the Magi* and, among the most common, *St. George and the Dragon*. The return to classicism appeared not only in the renewed use of orders but also in decoration: motifs such as candelabra, "grotesques" and medallions with heads of Roman Emperors, hermae, military friezes with hermae and coats of arms, festoons and putti were all popular. In the Baroque

A curved tympanum opening out like a fan, in Merida, Venezuela, set among the coffee plantations. Through colour, the simple plasterwork achieves impressive plasticity.

Partly covered by a hedge, this window in Sitges, Spain, is surmounted by collection of vases, volutes and fruit; the tympanum as such is "itemised" to make room for these elements.

The main door to the Cataldi mansion in Genoa, built at the end of the fifteen-hundreds, on the contrary, is courtly and sombre. Only the frieze reflects tradition, while other components modify classic rules to create new proportions.

The park of Drottningholms Castle, near Stockholm, boasts an admirable Chinese pavilion. Over and above the elegant two-colour decoration of the facade, each window is set off by a shallow tympanum and different Oriental faces.

The Moorish Giralda Villa, at L'Arboc, in Catalonia, built in the early part of the century. Doors and windows boast elegant Arab-style arches.

A curved tympanum in a palace in Damascus. The matching of two-colour stone with stylised flowers achieves impressive elegance.

Tympanums often incorporated shields and other insignia. This circular example stands over the entrance to a villa in Malta and is carved directly from the stone.

The Sanssouci villa at Potsdam, near Berlin, boasts a Tea Pavilion in the Chinese style.
Each window is arched and surmounted by an Oriental bust in the centre.

period, the compositional approach became more complicated and was embellished with mouldings and interrupted tympanums.

The interpretation of these elements became increasingly free. In Spain, Portugal and Latin America, the Baroque style was enriched with flourishing decoration inspired by the Iberian Churrigueresque manor.

Subsequently, and especially in the seventeen-hundreds, busts placed on top of the trabeation became very common, at times with an ovolo or echinus interrupting the tympanum, celebrating the owner of the villa.

Ultimately, new styles were imported from China, Egypt and other exotic places, which were used in alternation or else completely incorporated into the tympanums of classic architecture.

One of the most highly prized examples of Islamic art in Europe is undoubtedly the Alhambra in Granada.
In the fifteen-hundreds, the art of carving stone was well-known and works achieved considerable elegance, as in the case of this arched doorway.

Just like frontons, tympanums in Thailand also reach skywards; their shapes are mid-way between triangular and curved, and they are always characterised by intense use of colour.

Opposite page: a sinuous tympanum surmounting a window at Trujillo, Peru.

Attics

Dentils, moulding and small, twinned columns linked by stylised festoons are the characteristic features of this multi-coloured attic in Venezuela.

The Neo-Gothic Villa Elena at Valderice, near Trapani, is crowned by an attic recalling the merlons of Mediaeval castle-keeps; the entire villa is, in any case, inspired by Castillian architecture.

In earthenware, yet also often in mullioned and painted wood, these attics are typical of colonial mansions, forming a kind of crown which partly hides the roof.

An attic in Sana'a, Yemen. Here, architecture is known for a distinctly different tradition: this is a contemporary building where modern bricks are assembled and painted in an original fashion to create a pleasing decorative motif.

The modern definition of "attic" is a space or room, generally of limited height and area, inserted above the main cornice. Originally, however, the term was used for a low brick structure built on top of the cornice of the facade intended to hide the roof. Depending on periods, attics were variously decorated with balusters, statues, vases, mouldings, bands and all other kinds of embellishment designed to alleviate the composition. These additions include many elements that, although not exclusively belonging to this kind of structure, were used to decorate it, to the extent of becoming characteristic features.

Greek-style fretwork, also known as maze, is common to different cultures and its squared forms have also inspired textile decorations. The origins and meanings of this motif are unknown, although it has been suggested that the style refers to clasped hands. It is made up of sequences of lines developed by alternating straight lines and right angles. The result is a symmetrical, woven form where the basic motif may also be turned upside down, flanked by a mirror-image or rotated.

The compositional outlines may also include other motifs, such as sinuous sections, at times highlighted by simple colour contrast. In some examples, the swastika motif is used, originally a symbol of prosperity and rebirth which, repeated in sequence, resembles a maze. The reference to the labyrinth on the island of Crete, where the Minotaur symbolised the underworld, is very clear.

The wave motif, also known as a Greek or Vitruvian volute or continuous spiral, is a curvilinear version of geometrical fretwork. In some cases, it is integrated with central roses and leaves. On turning the corner of the building, this kind of unidirectional volute may "split" in the same or contrary directions.

The arabesque, or *guilloche*, is a decorative element which has retained its popularity over different periods and styles. The most frequent motif in the Renaissance and later times, it derives from various examples found in the interiors of Roman villas. It is comprised of knots and various other "interweaving" forms, creating two densely woven bands, which occasionally surround a row of disks. The bands may be overlapped or, in other cases, the

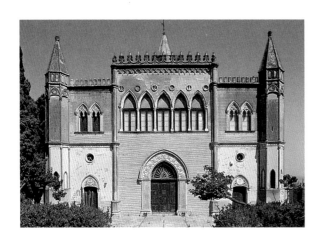

Contemporary architecture in Bahrein by no means forgets its traditional roots. Buildings – for the most part with roof-terraces – are set off by attics surmounting masonry parapets, thus hiding the terrace from the view of nearby buildings.

In the villas of the Knights of Malta, where security was always very important, mouldings and dentils were accompanied by arrow slits.

Even in Dubai, United Arab Emirates, terraced roofs are hidden from indiscreet observation by ethereal mullioned attics (side and below).

disks become rhombi. The central space often has a rosette. The repetition of the motif may be further elaborated with the inclusion of two rows of disks, by winding and scrolling the bands or by creating a series of loops. This style is common in numerous Islamic cultures.

The rosette, as well as being an element in complex decorative motifs, is also a motif in its own right and is frequent in all periods and cultures. The circular form has more or less abstract vegetal elements. In some cases, particular botanical species are depicted, both plants and flowers.

Paterae, very similar to rosettes, are more complex, larger, circular or oval decorative elements with a rosette in the centre. They derive from the broad bowls used in Roman religious ceremonies. They are in chalk or mosaic.

Attics – especially the simplest with a single transept, possibly decorated with rosettes or bas-reliefs – may be set off by urns, pines, spheres, vases and obelisks. Urns

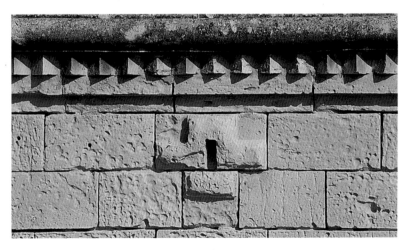

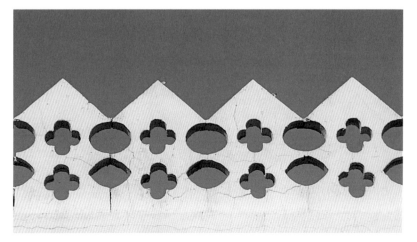

originally symbolised death, but soon came to have only a decorative meaning, just like pine-cones, characteristic of classic and, subsequently, Renaissance architecture. Spheres are also very common; they are depicted in a wide variety of forms, sometimes flattened into an oval shape.

Attics are not always decorated centrally and, at times, may have shields, coats of arms, clocks or trophies. The latter symbolised victory.

The ancient Greeks displayed the shields of defeated enemies on tree-trunks. Trophies were extended in Rome to include flags, drums and other military booty. Such groups, as interpreted in sculpture, were highly sought-after even in later periods, with the rediscovery of classic culture.

The courtly residences of Maracaibo date back to the late 1800s-early 1900s. The nouveaux riches copied from Europe, so that design is Neo-Classic while colour is entirely Caribbean

The same thing also happened in Miami Beach, where the Liberty style characteristic of the entire coastline of the city flourished enormously

Above: another example of a mullioned attic based on repetitive floral motifs.

Various motifs were developed to
decorate attics in different periods.
Side: two bas-reliefs, the first with
ovoli and honeysuckle leaves, the
second with various leaves and
convolvus flowers. They may be made
in earthenware, using moulds, or
stucco-work.

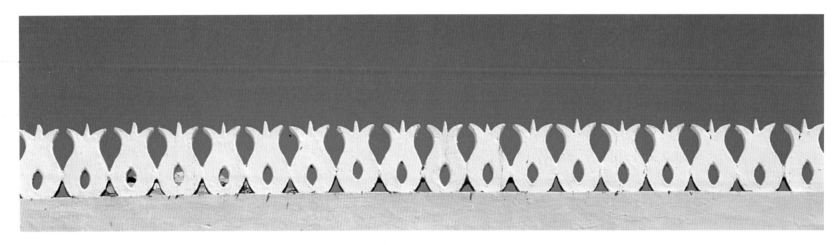

A series of mullioned amphora or bell-
shaped flowers (as the observer prefers)
tops the facade of this villa overlooking
the sea at Porto Cabello, Venezuela.

Two elegant bands of carved stone in
the wall, alternated with small simple
blocks of stone, crown the Ajakbash
Villa in Aleppo, Syria.

Extremely simple yet ensuring
considerable visual impact, this attic is
in a fortified villa at Sur, Oman. The
motif does not belong to local
tradition, nor does the informal use of
colour, yet the design blends gracefully
with the historic architecture of the
surroundings.

Gables

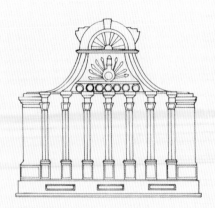

A structure raised above the level of the guttering to terminate the central section of the prospect of a building is called a gable (fastigium). The term originally referred to the sloping roof and the fronton, but its meaning was subsequently extended to embrace other elements such as the acroterium, the Gothic spire and various other vertical terminations of the facade introduced for decorative purposes. In some cases, gables bear inscriptions, noble coats of arms or even sundials and clocks.

They can be classified, much like frontons (to which they are closely related), into curved, stepped, Syrian, interrupted, Oriental and mixed styles. The curved gable perhaps originated in the Middle East or Egypt, but was utilised with some frequency only in Hellenic and Roman architecture. Retained by Byzantine architecture, gables re-appeared in monumental Venetian buildings in the early Renaissance.

With the Baroque age, gables came to be used extensively; designers displayed a certain predilection for this hallmark, which allowed imaginative formal variations always of considerable visual impact.

Stepped gables originated in the Gothic period and were especially frequent in residential architecture in northern Europe, were they enjoyed great popularity – particularly in Holland, which later exported the style to its colonies, from South Africa to Curaçao. The basic shape is triangular with the sloping sides resembling steps. In general, emphasis was given to elegant two-colour designs contrasting the exposed brickwork and main masonry of the building with the gable itself, made in different materials or plaster-work. The so-called Syrian gable appeared in the II century of the Christian age through the combination of two motifs already known in the Hellenic period: the niche-like fronton and the arched architrave. The Syrian gable was widely used in the architecture of the late Empire, and examples can still be seen today in the Near East, especially in Syria, where the style apparently originated.

When the gable is "broken" in the middle, it is said to be "interrupted". There are many variants of this hallmark; introduced at different times in different places, these variations

Above: tympanums, volutes, columns and cornices: every element is used to accentuate the skywards development of the facade.

Following pages: a Danish gable of the early 1900s in earthenware with volutes in stucco-work.
The two-colour design is particularly effective, thanks to the simplicity of the materials employed.

7

9

8

10

26

27

28

VILLA DETAILS

1

4

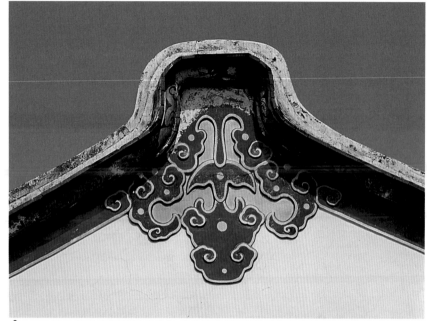

2

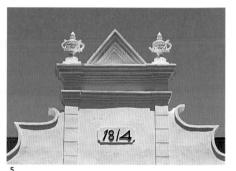

5

3

6

22   23   24   25

17

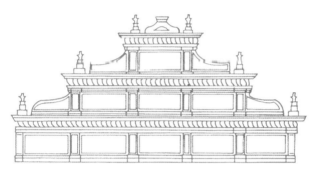

19

18

20

21

34

35

36

37

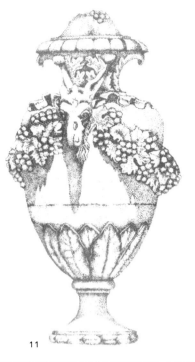

11

13

14

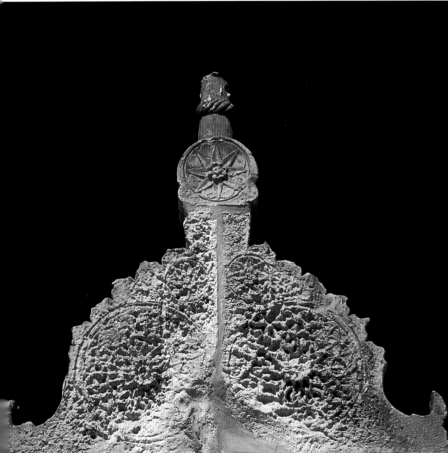

15

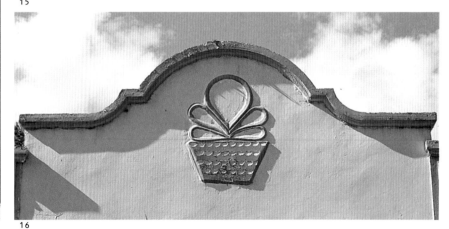

16

30

31

32

33

involve rather confused terminology, which differs from area to area. There are open or interrupted gables which, like frontons, may be interrupted on the converging sides. The interruption, which may involve any kind of gable, is made symmetrically along the vertical axis of the structure and is set off by the inclusion of coats of arms, busts, niches, scrolls, clocks and all kinds of other objects depending on the imagination of the designer. This was especially so in the colonies, where classic formal rigour was always blended with widespread freedom of design, in turn occasionally the source of new formal inventions. The gables of the Cape Dutch Style in South Africa are perhaps the most astonishing example. Never in Holland had there emerged such elegant and richly inventive designs.

The gable may project outwards on columns or shelves, with the trabeation on which it rests in a somewhat withdrawn position. The shape is not necessarily triangular or based on a triangle. The upper part may be curved and in this case the gable is said to be "cambered". The upper side may have a double curve or interrupted lines, both curved and straight. This example is typical of Baroque architecture. In this period, architects gave wings to their imaginations, inventing increasingly new and different styles − even to the extent of overlapping elements to produces gables within gables.

In the Orient, especially the Far East, these elements are rather rare and often confused with frontons. The complex frameworks that support roofs in the East are themselves decorations and the trend was increasingly towards highlighting rather than hiding them. True gables are found on the sides rather than on the facade, surmounting minor variations in the roofing.

There are many and varied examples in all times and all places. Effective expedients in terms of accentuating the courtly appearance of buildings and including characteristic elements, gables always had the ultimate objective of drawing the attention of passers-by and visitors to the facade of the villa. They accentuate the courtly nature of the architecture, reflecting the taste, culture and power of the owners of the villa.

Turrets

Since the dawn of time and in almost all cultures, mankind has built towers. Such reaching skywards is not only an attempt to extend horizons or vary the skyline. The sky has always been associated with spirituality. Paradise is in the sky, and even ancient temples once stood on stepped pyramids stretching skywards to the Heavens. The Ur ziggurat in Chaldea, is one of the first and best-known of these towers. It is no coincidence that the word "ziggurat" means "celestial mountain" or "mountain of the gods".

Such stepped structures developed into towers with many storeys, such as the legendary Tower of Babel, whose summit, according to the Bible, apparently "touched the sky". Similar towers were later built in veneration of divinities, a recurrent feature in most religions. In China, Japan, Korea and the Himalayan regions, holy towers – for the most part built of wood

Although standing next to the Royal Palace of Ayuttaya in Thailand, this turret has very little real association with local tradition; instead it recalls similar structures of European romanticism.

These somewhat fatuous turrets crown a contemporary building in Akureyri in Iceland. They culminate with a sphere and a conventional weather vane.

The observatory tower built in the park of the Royal Palace at Ayuttaya, the ancient capital of Thailand.

The pink stone of Jerusalem colours this austere turret built in the Neo-Mediaeval style in the Russian quarter of the historic city.

Strozzi mansion was built in the countryside near Rome in the XIV century. Streamlined towers characterises its outline, alternating with the narrow, defensive windows.

and brick – were extremely common. However, the most effective example of this desire is expressed in the imposing churches of the Gothic period, where each compositional element constantly thrusts upwards.

Materials were originally sun-baked bricks, still used today in the Yemen, and wood. Then, because of their greater strength, stone and earthenware were used in the building of this hallmark. Later, iron and then reinforced concrete were used.

The desire to dominate, at least from on high, was not typical only of religious buildings. The expression of power has always been one of the functions of architecture. This function is difficult to isolate, since it recurs in buildings of all kinds. However, there is no doubt that the elements that most evidently seek to express power and wealth are vertical in design. Thanks to such buildings, every civilisation proclaims its power and glory in forms which survive the civilisation itself and its descendants; the more consolidated

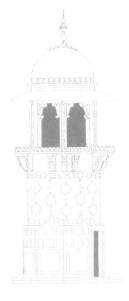

An observatory tower typical of Moghul architecture, common in India in between the XVI and XVII centuries. Always richly decorated, they often had vaulted roofs.

Below: at times, towers rise directly from the ground rather than surmount a building, as in the Villa Medicea at Cafaggiolo, near Florence; it also houses the main door.

and far-sighted the civilisation, the higher its architecture reaches to the sky.

Initially, turrets were intended to allow observation and control over the territory, to enable enemies to be identified in good time. They were later incorporated in fortified residences, the famous castles built all over Italy after the end of the Middle Ages, as well as in the Arab regions of the Near East. The height of the tower or turret, initially intended to impress attackers, now expressed the power and prestige of the owner.

The setting for stories of love and blood, these spartan structures soon fell out of favour with the aristocracy who, from the Renaissance, preferred living in much more comfortable surroundings. Consequently, towers, after a residential period, resumed their original function as places for observing the surrounding land, as well as, by exemplifying power, being formidable instruments of personal grandeur. In villas, towers and turrets were

Side: Mount Vernon, the seventeen-hundreds residence of George Washington, in Virginia, where this belvedere turret stands directly on the peak of the roof.

Top, centre: a tower in Muscat, Oman, located on the perimeter wall of a mansion.

Right: an elegant turret, inspired by classic forms but with an unmistakable tropical accent, setting off a contemporary mansion on the island of Lana'i, Hawaii.

preferably located in the centre or at the corners of the main facade. Central turrets are much more numerous and varied, with this kind of design flourishing particularly between the XV and XVIII centuries. The towers were suitable for living in and were frequently surrounded by balconies, which may themselves have been roofed. In eastern Europe, turrets were mostly surmounted by semi-spherical domes, whereas tapering spires were preferred in Middle Europe.

An unusual kind of turret is the so-called "wind tower", of Arab origin but common in Spain, which was strongly influenced by Islamic art. Its function was to enhance ventilation in the rooms below, generally the main rooms of the building. In contrast to the central turrets, corner turrets may project out from the line of the facade and are clearly inspired by the corner turrets of Mediaeval castles. Large and sturdy at the outset, they later evolved into more graceful and streamlined forms to become, in many instances, very similar to spires. Whether on the corners or in the middle of the facade, they are often decorated with clocks, sundials, coats of arms and inscriptions.

Delicate form and bold colours in this turret crowning the gardener's house in the park of Drottningholms Castle, on the outskirts of Stockholm.

Opposite page, top: half-way between a belvedere tower and a minaret, this example in Isfahan, Iran, has the unusual feature of oscillating when someone enters the building – the effect was apparently intended by the architect to impress guests.

Top: two examples of wind towers, the first in Doha, Qatar, the second in Saudi Arabia. These turrets exploit the laws of pneumatics to create natural ventilation in the rooms below by drawing air from them, thus creating a flow of cooler air from the narrow streets around the main building. Over and above their functional role, they all have highly compositional effects.

The imposing tower of Chignolo Po castle, near Pavia. First built in the Middle Ages, the castle was subsequently and frequently remodelled to improve comfort, and even the tower was turned into a graceful belvedere.

Roofs

One of the elements which best distinguishes villas in Thailand is the roof. Above: steep slopes, with ridges emphasised through different materials and colours, usually surmount white walls to enhance contrast.

Opposite page: the roof of the Berardo Palace in Madeira, also built using multi-coloured roofing tiles and a Korean roof, with slanted watersheds, painted antefix and ridges emphasised with raised portions.

Every building is surmounted and protected by a cover, which may be flat and therefore merely functional or may involve various kinds of slanted surfaces, which, through their design, effectively characterise the building itself. The best-known coverings are roofs and domes. The roof is a combination of elements, which, at various angles and variously inter-linked, surmount and protect the interior against atmospheric agents and climatic variations, at the same time as making a formal contribution to the appearance of the building. The structure of the roof may be separate from that of the main building or else be closely incorporated through a series of common structural elements.

Roofs can be divided into two types: flat roofs, mainly used in hot climates with little rainfall, and sloping roofs, common in temperate and cold climates, where the height of the ridge and the slope increase in proportion to the amount of rainfall and snow. Roofs are always designed and dimensioned in relation to local climatic conditions. The frequency and intensity of wind, rain and average winter snowfall are taken into account, while equally allowing a safety margin for extraordinary meteorological events.

Practical requirements have also influenced aesthetics, giving rise to new decorative elements; roofs with two slopes in ancient Greece saw the creation of the triangular fronton, which in turn became the typical element of classic facades, while in the Far East roof-slopes are slightly concave upwards. During the Renaissance, roofs evolved into new forms, especially in France where, thanks to the Mansard architects, roofs with several slopes were introduced with a loft underneath them. With the modern movement, owing to new technologies and materials, terraced roofs became common even in more temperate (and thus more rainy) latitudes.

The Latin word for roof is *tectum* ("covered"); as already mentioned, this element may take a variety of configurations closely related to the local climate. The majority of roofs share sloped surfaces, a load-bearing structure, a covering and a rainwater run-off system. The simplest type has two slopes (hut roofs), while four slopes are known as "pavilion roofs". A roof may even have only one slope. Slopes in general range between 12° and 60° and are obviously steeper in countries where winter snowfall has to be taken into account. In such

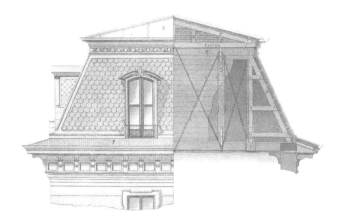

When roofs extend upwards and are covered by four slopes, the area underneath may be liveable and is called a loft or attic. The roof as such is limited to the small framework surmounting the attic itself.

A roof with four slopes and antique roofing tiles on the island of Lana'i, Hawaii.

The sinuous design of a Japanese roof, where only the ridge seems to be straight.

cases, the spaces between the ceiling of the last storey and the roof are exploited as lofts or attics, which may even be habitable and extend outside the roof structure as dormers and roof terraces. Attics have continuous watersheds or ridges, depending on the style chosen for their construction. The covering provides protection against atmospheric agents and is completely impermeable. Coverings may be thatch, wooden planks, bricks, cement or slabs of metal or stone. They are supported by a wooden or metal frame, involving a variety of beams, named in relation to their function: ridge, principle rafter, side post, ridge or collar beam, etc.

On the inside, these beams may be visible - as in the Mediaeval style - or hidden by a false ceiling.

While roof slopes in the West are always flat, in the East - especially the Far East - they are curved and concave upwards. In this case, there is no frame but a series of load-bearing elements supported by each other, which taper upwards towards the ridge, the highest point of the roof.

In Japan, but also in certain parts of China, this system is even more complex, with multiple, overlapping roofs, nevertheless built using the same system.

Four examples of ridged roofs. Different materials and colours combine distant periods and places. The colourful sheet metal roods in a village at Mahé, Seychelles. Below: the Caribbean Sea provides the background to the roofs of this mansion on the island of Tobago. Two pinnacles terminate one of the pavilions in Drottingholms Park, just outside Stockholm.
Right: a traditional residence in Indonesia. Style, static system and materials are utterly different to those of Western traditions, but this is precisely why the unusual profile is astonishing.

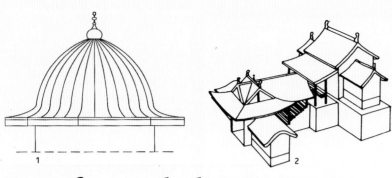

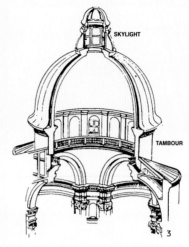

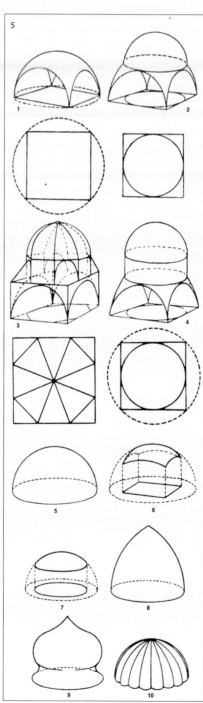

Roofs and domes

The most common roofing system in the Western world is the sloping roof with a load-bearing structure, a covering and accessories, such as guttering and roof-ridges. The system of wooden roofing structures in Oriental architecture, from China to Japan, is based on a simple principle which is nevertheless rather complex in terms of implementation. Unlike roof frames, which effectively function as beams placed on two supporting walls, the Oriental roofing system is based on the ability to make beams and supports solid with each other through very complicated joints (called tou-foung in Chinese). Since they have to withstand significant forces, these roofs may be very complex indeed, the more so as the roof becomes larger. Tou-foung is the most characteristic element of Oriental wooden architecture and may even assume sculptural forms. Its typical elements include: tien, a network of small beams, and chu, columns linked by beams and crosspieces. The area of the architrave provides a link between the roof, projecting significantly outwards, and the level of the

columns and wall, involving brackets which transmit the thrust forces generated by the overhanging system to the pillars. The system of wooden brackets (tou-kung) performs a function similar to that of the capital in classical architecture. Supported by pillars or columns, it comprises curved bracket arms surmounted by the architrave. As for Western orders, tou-kung equally displays different stylistic developments in different periods. Often repeated as a decorative motif even in masonry buildings, its original simplicity and functionality changed even to the extent of losing the load-bearing purpose. Roofs may be very varied. Stone is widely used as it is an historic material associated with local traditions. In general, quarries are nearby and even processing operations are performed locally. The slabs of stone are shaped, with a variable degree of precision in relation to the workability of the stone itself, which is cut into slabs of constant thickness and shape. Various installation techniques are used, depending on the local area. In general, the slabs are

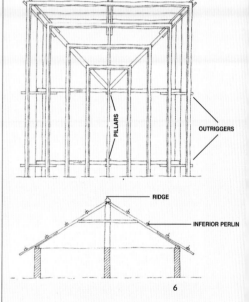

1. A copper roof.

2. The complex geometry of a Chinese roof.

3. A dome supported by pendentives with an illuminated tambour.

4. A double dome with a skylight over a square tower.

5. Various kinds of dome:
   1 crown,
   2 spherical pendentives,
   3 trumpeter,
   4 hemispherical on a tambour ,
   5 hemispherical,
   6 crown or Bohemian canopy,
   7 lowered,
   8 ogival,
   9 onion,
   10 pleated.

6. A trussed roof.

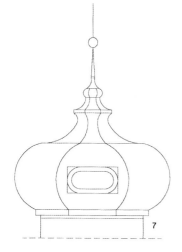

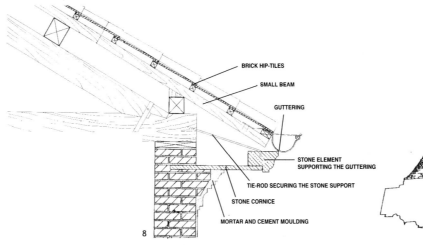

BRICK HIP-TILES

SMALL BEAM

GUTTERING

STONE ELEMENT
SUPPORTING THE GUTTERING

TIE-ROD SECURING THE STONE SUPPORT

STONE CORNICE

MORTAR AND CEMENT MOULDING

7

8

9

simply placed one on top of the other, although the first layer is occasionally secured with mortar or metal clamps. Today, for example, slate is secured in position by mechanical fastenings which require that each tile is drilled so that it can be riveted or secured with metal hooks. Brick roofs, with their typical earthenware colour, are the classical approach, used for centuries in all countries and every latitude. They offer good mechanical features and tend to develop a patina over time. The most common type in Antiquity was the Roman roofing tile: a simple, flat tile with raised edges and a trapezoidal geometry to permit overlapping installation and also facilitate rainwater run-off. The ridges and joints between these tiles were covered by hip-tiles, a curved element which could also be used on its own – as seen in roofs from the Middle Ages down to our own times. Ceramic roofing materials are not a modern innovation, although they are rather unusual in private homes. Many churches in northern Europe, Spain and the Orient adopt this system. The aesthetic result is distinctly

different to that produced with stone or earthenware: it is possible to create colourful spans and varied geometries. These tiles are generally hexagonal, square or rectangular. The so-called "pottery" tiles have a white base paste and a less porous, increasingly more compact structure depending on the base paste used and the curing temperature. They are generally vitrified to ensure they are impermeable. Installation involves a thin layer of mortar. Among metals used for roofing applications, copper is particularly common. It is very durable and withstands atmospheric and corrosive agents very well; it is also very easy to work, when either hot or cold. It can be modelled into any shape and is excellent for joints. Over time, its colour changes to sea-green and brown. Copper roofs can be utilised in a wide variety of situations, including steep slopes and onion domes. It was once installed in large plates, whereas today it is cut from coils into strips at the building site.

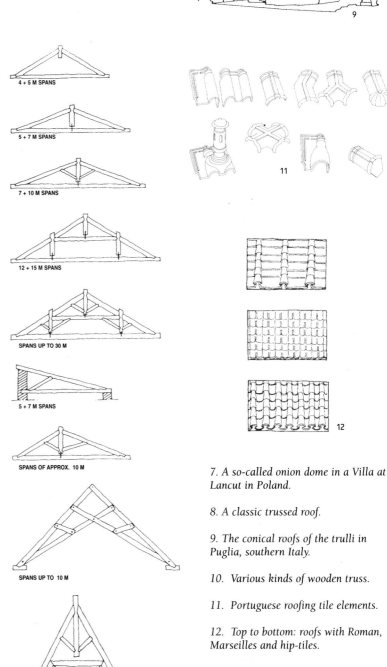

4 + 5 M SPANS

5 + 7 M SPANS

7 + 10 M SPANS

12 + 15 M SPANS

SPANS UP TO 30 M

5 + 7 M SPANS

SPANS OF APPROX. 10 M

SPANS UP TO 10 M

5 + 7 M SPANS

10

11

12

7. A so-called onion dome in a Villa at Lancut in Poland.

8. A classic trussed roof.

9. The conical roofs of the trulli in Puglia, southern Italy.

10. Various kinds of wooden truss.

11. Portuguese roofing tile elements.

12. Top to bottom: roofs with Roman, Marseilles and hip-tiles.

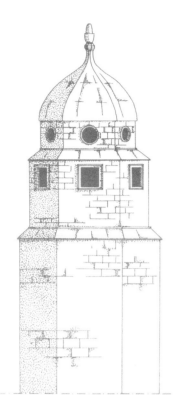

Domes

The latin word for dome is cupula (barrel). Domes are a curved, more or less regular roof covering, with a circular, square or polygonal structure. Domes represent two ideas: from the outside, they resemble a globe, while from the inside they are a miniature celestial vault. Celestial and human dimensions interact once again through architecture – the faithful mirror of the ambitions and aspirations, both earthly and idealistic, of mankind.

A dome is defined by the rotation of a curve (which is not necessarily a portion of a circle) around a vertical axis. Its cross-section may thus be hemispherical, semi-elliptical or a parabolic arc. From the point of view of statics, domes discharge their load thrusts on to the support masonry's vertical and lateral components; for this reason, such masonry must be very sturdy and at times even requires lateral buttresses. Domes may be smooth or have crowns and pendentives: these elements are especially used when the dome is not built over a circular base. The element linking the dome and the base is the tambour. Depending on their shapes, domes have numerous other names or descriptions: spherical, hemispherical, flattened, elongated, ogival, bulb or onion, pendentive, crowned or bayed. When the area to be covered is not square, a tambour is inserted between the dome and its impost, performing a linking function. Among the various kinds of dome, one of the most curious is the so-called bulb or onion dome, associated with Islamic architecture but also to be found in certain buildings in Spain and Portugal.

Pseudo-domes were also very common among ancient civilisations – whether in the Mediterranean, the East or Mesa America; they were false domes built using stone ashlars placed one on top of the other in gradually descending diameters until they met at the peak (as in the "nuraghi" of Sardinia or the "trulli" of Puglia). Yet it was the Romans who studied and classified the building systems used in true domes, where the ashlars are supported by a framework until the last stone is installed, thereby terminating the system of thrust forces and only at this stage becoming self-supporting.

The first domes were in brick and derived from the Etruscan arch; later, the Romans introduced a decisive improvement with the widespread use of cement. This evolution

A polygonal dome built in the second half of the 1500s in Cambridge, Great Britain. It surmounts a six-sided tower and is topped by a pinnacle.

Zanzibar was for a long time a colony and even the capital of the Sultanate of Oman. Arab architecture is frequent. This semi-circular dome stands on top of an hexagonal base without a tambour.

Opposite page, top: the drawing of one of the many domes in Istanbul; divided into 24 veils, it is topped by a pinnacle and supported by columns.

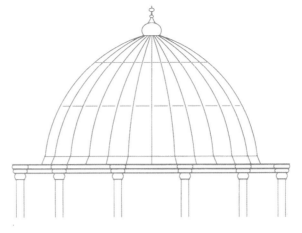

Left: the familiar appearance of this dome should not be taken for granted – Rome is far away! This villa is actually in Puerto Vallarta, on the Pacific coast of Mexico.

Natchez, on the Mississippi and bordering with Tennessee, has many cotton plantations. The prevailing style is neo-Classic but it is by no means rare to find Moorish influences, as here in Longwood House, set off by an onion dome.

Below: a series of domes with skylights embellishes the residential skyline in Puerto Vallarta, Mexico.

reached its peak in the time of Emperor Hadrian and the structural system often influenced the entire architectural project: the structure became lighter with the inclusion of brick amphora or ribbing, especially for the imposts; load-bearing arches were introduced, as well as flying buttresses and niches. This system was later admirably adopted in Byzantine architecture, which gave considerable impulse to the use of domes, which after 1000 years came once again to be used in Europe.

A flattened, ogival dome in Kashan, Iran, entirely in stone; exterior simplicity is offset by rich decoration inside.

Baranow Castle, Poland has many towers each topped by superimposed domes; the uppermost dome is rather like a skylight.

Below: a curious, eclectic dome on the corner of a mansion in Antananarivo, Madagascar.

Left: a close-up of the dome decorated with multi-coloured tiles, Giralda Villa at L'Arboc, near Barcelona.

Right: the interior of the dome over the main hall of the Sukias Villa in the Armenian quarter of Isfahan, Iran, where wealthy merchants once lived.

The skylight of the Azem Villa, Hamah, Syria, stands on top of a semicircular dome and is itself completed by a small ogival dome.

Side: a fine example of an onion dome terminating a tower. It is part of a 1600s mansion in Kazan, Russia.

Spherical domes embraced by octagonal cladding are typical of the Romanesque age. In the Gothic period, domes became more complex and streamlined over the ribbed cross vault.

In the Renaissance, as buildings grew in size, the double dome was introduced (with a blind area inside): one dome supported the roofing and the other the internal decoration. In this period, there were also spherical domes with meridian ribbing, whereas the Baroque age saw the spread of domes with an elliptical plan, as developed in exemplary manner by Borromini. Moreover, the true Baroque dome culminates with a skylight, which provides illumination for the interior. The interior decoration of domes has its own distinct traditions. Paintings, mosaics, bas-reliefs, stone and stucco ribbing (true and imitation) and delicate stone mullions embellish many examples. The Romans decorated their invention with caissons with rose emblems in the centre. Ribbing was introduced by Gothic architecture.

In the Near and Middle East, domes were extremely important and the equally important decoration of interiors involved famous mosaics made of tiny vitreous earthenware tiles, widely used from Isafan to Samarkand. Even Neo-Classic architects exploited the potential of domes, introducing ribbed rose emblems in the interior.

Domes with steel frameworks began to appear in the 1800s, followed by lattice-work with triangular and four-sided frames culminating in the geodetic dome.

Spires, pinnacles and chimneys

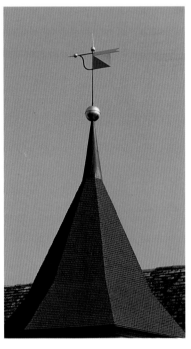

The facade of the eighteenth century Pomarchao Villa in Portugal is set off by a series of vases with pinnacles that emphasise the vertical impact of the composition.

A spire with a wind vane, Flaatch Castle, Switzerland.

Tall spires and more modest pinnacles are the decorative elements that most emphasise the vertical development of a building. Shaped like pyramids or extremely tapered with pointed tips, they were very popular in the Gothic period, not the least because of their important static function in stabilising the bold, especially religious, architecture of the 1200s-1300s. Once embraced by residential designs, they became purely decorative elements symbolising power and prestige. They were extensively developed during the Renaissance when common pyramidal and conical styles were joined by more elaborate designs resembling amphora.

The classic example of such hallmarks is the acroterium, from the Greek *akrotérion*, meaning "summit" or "highest point". They were installed on the peak and side extremities of the fronton, although the term, by now used for the entire decoration, originally referred only to the base. The first examples were painted disks of terracotta, followed by three-dimensional compositions with motifs inspired by Nature, with vases and mythological figures such as "Winged Victory". Vitruvius defined them as "sculptures placed above temples", since they were initially found only in such buildings. He suggested that those installed at the sides be half the height of the tympanum and those crowning the peak one-eighth larger than these. These elements have decorative as well as apotropaic functions.

In many examples, the key positions in the pronaos and fronton are taken by obelisks. These have a single drum of granite or other hard stone, with four sides tapering slightly towards the tip covered with inscriptions. Obelisks are often surmounted by a pyramidal cusp, which is, at times, faced with metal to reflect sunlight.

They date from Ancient Egypt, although they were also used in other civilisations with various religious and civil meanings. The later examples were inspired by the huge obelisks of Ancient Egypt, few of which are still to be found in their original sites, especially in the wake of Napoleonic plundering which saw them installed in the squares and gardens of many European cities. Obelisks crown the facades of many 1600s-1700s villas in alternation with statues, vases and spheres. In Italy, this is especially true for the villas of the Veneto and certain examples in Lombardy.

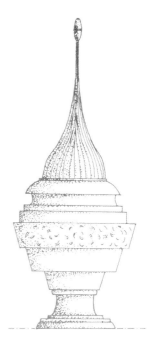

Spires are very common in the Orient. This spire, entirely faced with gold leaf, stands over the Royal Palace in Bangkok.

Vases with spires became common in Europe during the Mannerist period. They were included in villa facades of decorated garden avenues.

Even a simple wind vane may resemble a pinnacle. The example here in wrought iron stands on the roof of Mount Juliet Manor in Ireland.

An elaborate chimney-piece in the Mariiuskie Palace, Moscow, built in 1688. Although essentially functional elements, chimneys nevertheless also acquired decorative effects.

Above: a pinnacle topping a roof in Chiang Mai, northern Thailand. It has a small gilt spire surrounded by concentric circles.

A painted terracotta pinnacle highlights the corner of a facade of a mansion in Singapore.

Above, right: twinned chimneys in a Scottish manor house. High rainfall means that even the chimneys need small roofs, with short spires to streamline the design.

Opposite page, centre: a set of chimneys in a country home in Madeira. The stacks are grouped to create a decorative motif.

Spread: an elaborate spire in wrought iron proudly standing over a manor near Aberdeen, Scotland.

Spheres in stone, marble, earthenware, cement or – more rarely – metal usually finish off the facades of 1600s-1700s villa in alternation with vases, pine cones and obelisks. Statuary art, urns and vases are the most important elements in emphasising the vertical prospect of villas. One of the reasons why these elements are so popular is their enormous adaptability to any kind of proportion and decorative motif without ever losing their circular symmetry.

The fascination of these elements is based on their origins: they were used to hold the ashes of the dead, a role which has always given them mystical connotations. With the rediscovery of Classic architecture, especially in Mannerism, they were used again on a large scale.

In the 1700s-1800s, their popularity was enormously enhanced by the engravings of Piranesi, who skill made every Roman relic supremely interesting.

Dovecotes are a particularly kind of roofing element, which also date back to the Romans. They were very common in country homes, where they symbolised an important aspect of rural economy. The doves flew in and out through tight and narrow slits, while the keepers climbed up from the inside on steep steps above the ceiling. There were also ducts for providing the birds with fresh water.

Chimneys are other elements that emphasise the vertical impact of buildings. These include the smoke-stack as such, which draws combustion fumes away from the roof, and the

Solid and imposing, this chimney in a 1700s villa in the Brianza area, northern Italy, is a major element characterising the whole building

Right: another chimney in Madeira. The smoke stack has a mobile duct which follows the wind, thanks to the horse wind vane, to improve drawing.

chimney pot, preventing infiltration by rainwater and ensuring a good draw even in windy conditions through special devices – which may be fixed, mobile or even support a wind vane.

Ridges and eaves

When function becomes design: eaves offer designers a whole range of opportunities. The curved design of Oriental roofs is particularly ideal for such purposes. Top: a corner element on a roof in Poun, South Korea, where the guttering is emphasised by a sequences of antefixes. Bottom: another corner-piece, this time in Kaohsiung, Taiwan, with an enamelled earthenware decoration.

Just as a good suit needs a hat, so a fine building needs a worthy roof. Roofs are ideal for stately and artistic interpretations, although the most noticeable elements are ridges and guttering. They are the beginning and the end, the summit and the link with the rest of the building – and villa architects have certainly never overlooked such design opportunities.

The ridge of a roof is the joint between two slopes. They are either watersheds or "valleys" depending on the rainwater run-off. Ridge tiles, having a wide variety of shapes and sizes, may be placed over the ridge or watershed. When roofs have four or more slopes, or domes, the ridge is variously highlighted by elements which tend to accentuate the vertical prospect of the building. These include turrets and spires, as well as statues and, in Oriental cultures, the *chapsang*, the guardians of the house, whose threatening appearance is linked with legends and myths.

While the ridge is the uppermost part of the roof, the eaves are the lowest point; they may be straight or protrude beyond the outer walls of the building. The edge is called the eave-line and is often decorated with cymatiums and antefixes. The former, from the Greek *kymátion* ("small wave"), are small, undulating mouldings crowning the cornice of the eaves themselves. The most frequent decorative motif is aligned antefixes. From the Latin *antefixum* ("secured in front"), these are triangular or semi-circular terracotta (or stone or marble) plaques decorating the heads of the roofing tiles, the bases or the tympanum and the eave-line itself. They were probably first used in wooden buildings to protect the trabeation against humidity. They may be painted or decorated in relief with a variety of mythological, plant and animal figures, as well as human-like figures as in Greek culture. At times, they have a twin volute surmounted by small palm trees. The antefix was later employed, with simpler and repetitive decorations, in Etruscan and Roman architecture and is still a frequent element in the traditional architecture of the Far East.

Although not categorised (as for orders), they can be outlined as Doric, rather simple and generally only painted; Ionic, with an oval and convex shape; or Lesbos, with curved surfaces decorated with heart-shapes. Depending on the kind of villa, the antefixes may be in wood, exposed or plastered and decorated in a variety of ways. In general, stately architecture in the

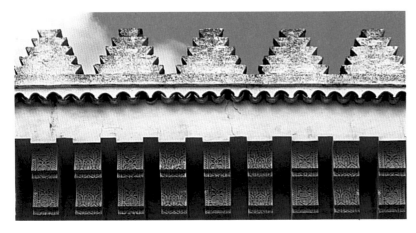

*Strong impact yet extremely simple:
these eaves in Marrakesh have regular,
small and well-shaped wooden beams
supporting miniature arches and
stepped pyramids.*

*Swirling, decorated ridges seemingly
supporting the sky characterise this
roof in Taipei.*

Ridges are not always straight. Oriental roofs often have curved ridges, as here in Kaohsiung, Taiwan.

Classic eaves in European architecture viewed from below. The beams overhang and, once stuccoed, they, themselves, form a decorative motif. There is a band with dentils close to the joint with the load-bearing wall.

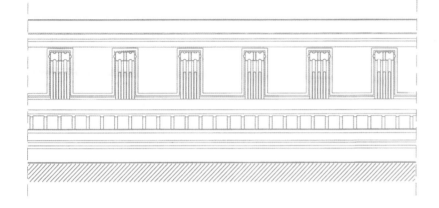

West uses antefixes in earthenware, which are stuccoed and decorated with stylised floral designs inside squares and circles.

Similar functions are performed by wooden borders with dentils, used in the tropical mansions of European colonists especially in the Caribbean, India and Indo-China. They prevent heavy rainfall seeping underneath the roof and are also an elegant decoration. They are effectively thin strips of fret-worked wood with tooth-shaped pieces on the lower edge that facilitate rainwater run-off. Even the area under the eaves may be decorated in various ways, depending on the materials used. In Central Asia, colourful paintings with floral and geometrical motifs are common.

Dentils and rosettes are more common beneath the eaves in Europe, and are clearly of classical inspiration. In traditional Oriental architecture, eaves are arched upwards. This effect involves adding elements at the eave-line which – since they

An intricate terracotta chapsang standing guard over a villa in Hong Kong. This tradition is still very common today and every home has its guardian.

Opposite page, top: eaves at Taegu, South Korea. The wooden structure is visible and elegantly painted.

are now visible – embellish the composition.

The exterior outline is also modified. Monotonous horizontal lines are abandoned and – by raising the eaves, the corners of the roof and, at times, even the line of the ridge – roofs become less austere and more delicate.

Centre: eaves in Damascus. Again, the tastefully decorated wooden structure is clearly visible.

A delicate lace-like pattern in fret-worked wood highlights the eaves of this two-sloped roof in Colombo, Sri Lanka.

Above: when the roof has several slopes, the ridge is no longer a line but a meeting-point which can be emphasised in many ways. This Irish manor house has a type of skylight illuminating the room below.

Spouts

Rainwater flows out of the mouth of a winged monster in this building in Prambanan (Indonesia). The block of carved stone is linked to the rainwater collection system and ensures that it drops well away from the building.

Another spout, also winged but in wrought iron, allows rainwater run-off in a mansion in Merida, Venezuela.

SPOUTS (the Latin word for these is "*pluvia*" meaning "rain") collect rainwater from the guttering, placed immediately underneath the roof covering so that water running off the slopes of the roof itself does not splash on to the cornice. Guttering may be fixed or mobile, have various cross-sections, be hidden or on view. Rainwater guttering and spouts can be made from earthenware, iron, copper, galvanised sheet metal and plastic.

Spouts direct rainwater from the guttering to the drains. At times, they are encompassed within the masonry of the building, although they are also frequently left on view or are free-fall types, simply allowing water to drop freely to the ground below away from the wall. Such spouts are an interesting aspect of this particular detail, since in the past they were very common and elaborately decorated. They were given animal and human designs long before drains were invented. In certain parts of South East Asia, where rainfall is regular all year round, there are special systems known as chain spouts. The normal outlet is fitted with a metal chain that directs water towards collection tanks or drain ducts, avoiding lateral splashing. Spouts may be secured to the walls with brackets and collars, which can equally be highly decorative. If discharge at ground level is simply on to the surface rather than directly into drains, the tip of the mouth may be flat (if linked by a simple coupling to ground level) or T-shaped, when the spout has a holed perpendicular insert that sprays rainwater throughout its length. The technical names of spouts are highly imaginative: "storks" are the brackets which support the guttering, "staples" are a kind of tie-rod performing the same function, and "heads" mark off the start and end of guttering sections. Despite their highly functional purpose, all these details play a significant role in the overall decoration of a villa.

Left: a linking element between spouts transforms a practical device into decoration.

Below: this duct-shaped spout protrudes from the walls of the ancient city of Cusco, Peruvian Andes.

Bottom: a similar design approach in Bilad a Sur in Oman, except that this spout is made of wood rather than earthenware.

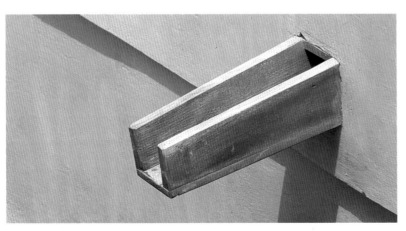

Top: a vaguely Oriental combined with European wrought iron work in this dragon-shaped rain spout in Wenkenhof Castle, Richen, Switzerland.

Centre: a spout carved in the typical local pink stone projects between the arches of this portico in Jerusalem.

Above: graceful, projecting outwards, slender yet strong: this spout is in a courtyard in Aleppo, Syria. Skilfully carved in stone, it reproduces the decorations of the tympanums and the storey-markers.

Lookout turrets

An isolated turret along the garden wall of the Villa Allegri (Grezzana, province of Verona, Italy): the villa itself dates from the 1600s but the turret belongs to an earlier, 1500s mansion.

Jutting out into the sea, this turret ensured excellent visibility for sentries along the bastions of the Spanish fort at Rabat, Morocco.

TURRETS were originally tiny structures providing shelter for sentries located along patrol routes or the entrances to military buildings. Today, they may even indicate a guard-house or, at times, a bartizan (from the Latin *brittisca* meaning "winter home"). From the X century, they developed into a small wooden or masonry structure with a square or rectangular base projecting from merlons or else they were built on top of fortified walls and had similar purposes as the machicolation, often complete with embrasures. The latter were defensive elements, originally horizontal slits for crossbowmen, then vertical for archers and, later still, round for riflemen. These arrow-slits were sometimes inter-linked and splayed towards the inside to ensure easier weapon handling and a wider field of fire. They were naturally placed in the most strategic positions, both for better defence and a better view. In more isolated regions, moats may have placed round the turrets, as in ancient medieval castle keeps, though they were possibly more like pleasant lakes, while few trees were planted around them to avoid giving shelter to attacking forces.

Villa turrets maintain this defensive character but, since castle-like sieges were unlikely, they developed into a protected observation post overlooking the surrounding land (although retaining arrow-slits in the eventuality of armed conflict). They were generally accessible from the first floor (the noble floor), often directly from the main hall or, in any case, from the rooms nearest the corners of the building offering the best views around the villa itself. Turrets are always rather small (for just one sentry) and roofed to provide shelter in the event of permanent surveillance. Their spartan design leaves little room for decoration. The support shelf is often made up of overlapping concentric circles, a conical stone element or overhanging beams projecting from the main walls of the building.

The roof shape is determined by the generally circular cross-section of the turret, which thus requires a bell-shaped or round dome, often topped by a sphere. In certain examples, the body of the turret – usually jutting out from the main building – continues down to ground level rather like a bastion, giving the villa a fortified appearance. Turrets were used for defence against the pirates and bands of robbers infesting the seas and countryside last century. This was when the turret enjoyed its "golden age" in residential buildings, having formerly been

The bracket supporting this turret on the exterior of a castle in Stockholm is decorated to the point of becoming the most eye-catching element.

Left: an elegant turret near Lagos, southern Portugal, built in local stone and made less austere by the domed roof, the strips of stone and the elegant moulding.

Above: a palace in Mgarr, Malta. The walls surrounding the courtyard are fortified with defensive turrets and towers, which were only embellished at a later stage.

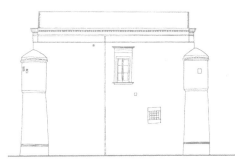

The fortified Sordo farmhouse at San Severo, Puglia, southern Italy, has circular structures at the four corners halfway between towers and turrets.

Gravina, province of Bari: the Pellicciari fortified mansion has gracious turrets supported by two brackets.

built only in castles and fortresses. Throughout southern Italy, for instance, there are fortified farmhouses overlooking olive groves, vineyards and almond orchards.

In the same way, in the rest of the Mediterranean area and certain parts of Latin America, both along the coast and in the interior, turrets were built on the corners of more isolated buildings, clearly demonstrating a need for security lacking in other, more accepted ways.

On the one hand, owners required comfortable, airy and elegant homes but, at the same time, they could not ignore the need for safety imposed by isolated locations often very distant from towns and villages.

As time passed, this detail became more elegant and the original designs, already modified from their initial applications in castles, were softened even further, thereby transforming a utilitarian structure into yet another decorative opportunity. They were, nevertheless, inspired by military structures. Standing over sheer cliffs, in open fields or city squares, turrets are both defensive and a declaration, exemplifying both times of trouble and economic power, even to the point of turning a stronghold into a distinctive detail.

Quinta Anauco, built on the outskirts of Caracas by cocoa plantation owners last century has turrets on all sides, testimony of troubled times even in the cities.

Bottom left: a turret in Valetta, Malta. Built entirely in local stone, it is topped by an ogival dome and sphere.

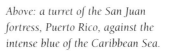

Above: a turret of the San Juan fortress, Puerto Rico, against the intense blue of the Caribbean Sea.

Above, right: this town house in a village in Catalonia also has a corner turret to keep an eye on events in the vicinity.

Stairways

Large and small stairways were added to villas. They took varied and fanciful forms: huge staircases rising to the noble floor in residence of the Lord of the Manor, as well as those smaller ones in parks and gardens between terraces and embankments, decorated with volutes, vases, balusters and statues. They highlighted the fundamental architectural and landscape compositions of the villas.

Reaching skywards has always been one of the great aspirations of mankind and architecture expresses this desire in many ways. Thus a series of juxtaposed steps to be climbed on foot (and even on horseback) is soon transformed from a functional element into a fundamental, celebratory statement. This is especially true of the Renaissance, when stairways were a major component in architectural compositions. In villas, they particularly took on the important role of providing access to the noble floor, as a means of celebrating the culture or the opulence of their owners.

Such vertical links were increasingly accentuated, until the static geometries of Palladian villas in the Baroque Age exploded in a huge variety of compositions. Between the 1600s and the 1700s, the theme was developed extensively and combined with statuary and landscape arts to wonderful effect.

While the 1800s were a period of relative inventive stasis, the Art Déco or Liberty period brought back the taste for the unusual and the original with volutes and balusters assembled in new and exciting combinations.

Today, as in the past, stairways and steps provide a perspective which emphasises an entrance or an avenue. Taste and technique can turn such functional, repetitive and monotonous elements into characteristic additions: the great designs of the past suggest endless possibilities and alternatives, expedients and materials that still inspire designers and owners. Staircases also include steps (wider and lower) and ramps (effectively simple slopes). There are many variants: frontal, strictly in line with the main entrance; basement, more common in religious buildings; and lateral, on one side of and parallel to the main building. Those in line with the main entrance may have a single ramp, with or without landings, or open out

A delicate stairway leading to the noble floor of the Lugisland Villa in Rabat, Malta. The initial single set of steps opens out like a pair of tongs to embrace a small terrace.

There is nothing better than a broad stairway to accentuate the approach to a mansion. This one at Godi Valmarana Villa at Lonedo di Lugo, near Vicenza, Italy, is several dozen metres long and is interrupted by a number of flat sections.

Even in the colonies, broad stairways highlight the villas of the conquistadores – as in this semi-circular example at Herreria, a few kilometres from Quito, Ecuador.

Below: this apparently Baroque staircase in local pink stone on the road to Bethlehem, with ashlars recalling the Mannerist style, is actually a recent building in Palestine.

Below, right: the main staircase to one of the temples in Prambanan, Indonesia, the inspiration for many similar staircases throughout the area.

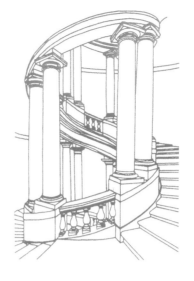

This voluptuous spiral staircase in the Caprarola Villa near Viterbo, Italy, was designed by Vignola in the late-1500s.

Opposite page, top: a simple staircase in Tai Fu Tai Village, Hong Kong.

Below: a multi-coloured staircase in Trinidad. The simplicity of form is offset by the rich colours.

like a pair of tongs with two sets of steps, generally having a straight section and a curved portion.

One of the major features of this detail is the slope, defined by the ratio between the depth and height of the steps, in turn distinguished as more or less steep steps and stairs. Staircases may thus be "slow" or "fast", depending on how quickly a person can walk up (or down) them. There may even be flat areas or landings between sets of steps. At times, the transition between two parallel ramps is continuous,

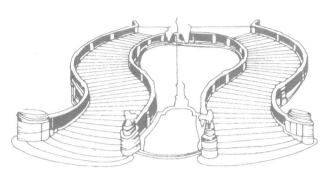

A twin staircase – typical of the entire Baroque period, with volutes and with or without landings – is usually marked off by elegant balusters.

Below: form and colour accentuate these short steps in front of a house in Chiang Mai, northern Thailand.

with a fan of steps rotated through 180° in a progressive curve. Stepped staircases have a steeper tread gradient. Each step may require a single or several footsteps, whatever the height.

The most common materials used in Italy are marble, various kinds of granite and local stone, such as *pietra serena* and pietra forte in Tuscany, travertine in Latium or "cipollino" in the Veneto. Less ambitious staircases may have terracotta tiles, as frequently seen throughout the Mediterranean. In the colonies, wood successfully took the place of European marbles, although local stone materials are also common.

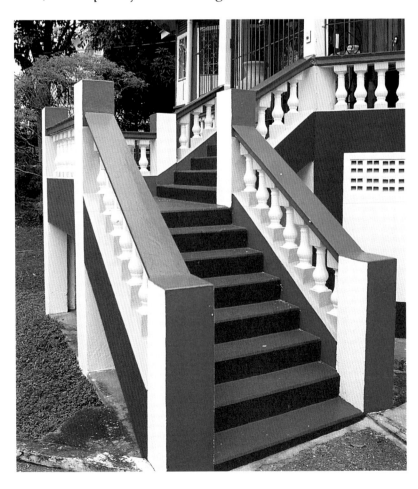

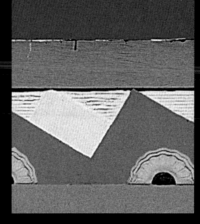

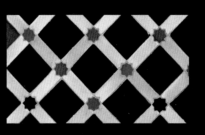

Art and beauty

Not everything that is beautiful is art. And not everything that is artistic is necessarily beautiful. Art is a form of visual communication and beauty a question of taste and judgement, which are difficult to define with ordinary yardsticks. Architecture may be both. Form, dimensions and the base colour or overall chromatic effect combine to give character to a facade. Colour is effectively an integral part of form, communication and architecture, even when it creates non-existent elements or false shadows. Trompe-l'oeil even "dematerialises" solid walls, dissolving them into delightful and vital visions. Backgrounds evolve through refined mirroring of real life and imitation artefacts, of the observer and the scene observed, just as bas-reliefs become "frons scenae", a band narrating deeds and stories, usually celebrating the patron. Masques take on unusual human, animal and even diabolical outlines. Dream-like or mythological elements thus become part of the decoration of villas, alongside motifs inspired by Nature, in the form of festoons, medallions and garlands. Even forms inspired by classical tradition owe their success to the patient copying work of Renaissance and Baroque architects and essayists who turned the "Grand Tour" in Rome into a fundamental fact-finding occasion. The engravings of Giovan Battista Piranesi, for example, played a decisive role in creating the Romantic taste for ruins, where classical elements appear as if rediscovered after being long-forgotten. Gardens, both natural and artfully like Nature, surround these mysterious places, in engravings as in reality. Mansions seem as if engulfed and devoured by vegetation, their size and design obscured, transformed into green architecture, a new kind of landscaping art. Fruit, vegetables and military trophies blend with aristocratic coats of arms – the traditional signs of ownership, ancient origins, family relationships and privileges. Forged iron joins carved stone and baked clay in defining the details of villas. Equally, mosaics, azulejos and majolica link East and West, Byzantium and Rome, Islam and Christianity through villa details.

Colour

IT IS WIDELY BELIEVED that every form is initially neutral and is only coloured afterwards through dyeing. Colour is thus viewed as an accessory, to be applied to the object in order to personalise it in line with individual taste. In truth, form and colour develop hand in hand. There are even animal species that survive thanks to their colour: frightening, protective or attractive, depending on circumstances and necessity. Colour is entirely a visual means of communication and representation and, in the facades of buildings, also a protective coating that helps safeguard masonry against atmospheric agents and the wear and tear of time.

Colour is the result of selective reflection of light of certain wavelengths. Colours may be bright or dull, light or dark, shiny or opaque, soft or intense. Colour is a visual sensation but in facades also acquires a tactile role. Surfaces may be shiny or opaque, matt or smooth, rough, porous or velvety.

The chromatic composition of a facade is important because it significantly influences visual perception and memory of architecture. Colour improves recollection of a building and influences personal taste and judgements.

Since Antiquity, emphasis has always been given to the harmony of colours: with each other and the landscape (earth, rock, sand), the lay of the land itself (plains, hills, mountains, coastlines) and even climate (sunny, windy, rainy, foggy). The chromatic composition of a facade is dictated by the natural, permanent colours of materials and colours superimposed on large surface areas.

There may be more or less subtle distinctions of colour between backgrounds, cornices, reliefs and decorations. This combination is called "the base colour", i.e. the overall visual perception of individual colours. Yet colour is also very alive: it not only changes with the light, humidity and time but may even be used to suggest non-existent depth, shadow and sunlight in dark places, architectural decoration and reliefs in plain walls.

With trompe-l'oeil, walls came to life, masonry de-materialised and space was entirely re-invented: supreme examples are the frescoes in the Roman villas of Pompeii, the early perspectives of Masaccio and Brunelleschi and the frescoes of Mantegna and Giulio Romano. Physical barriers disappeared to create "virtual" visions capturing the attention of observers.

Spanish colonial architecture at times blends superbly with native artistic traditions, giving rise to evocative compositions. Colour often acquires a formal role, as in this two-coloured facade in Trujillo, Peru.

The intense colours of Caribbean architecture reflect the sea, Nature, fruit and fabrics. Maracaibo, northern Venezuela, is wonderful example.

Akureyri, near the northern coast of Iceland: the sun is a rare visitor and then only in summer. Architecture, and mansions in particular, embrace fascinating colours that compensate for the generally black and white landscape

Miami Beach: early-1900s Art Déco uses unthinkable colours for the Old Continent. Once again, these colours are inspired by the sun, the sea and the luxurious vegetation of the hinterland.

At times, colour is not merely an "added value" but an illusory form of architecture. Trompe-l'oeil ensures grandeur in otherwise plain settings, depth in narrow places and creates "villas" from mere "houses".

With the great flourishing of this form of art in the 1600s-1700s, space expanded, suggesting new worlds and revealing unknown horizons.

Design solutions were sometimes playful. Artists depicted the cultivated atmosphere of humanist salons, where princes commissioned paintings of those objects which best interpreted their virtues, interests and deeds. Yet these artists did not overlook the more prosaic vices, traits and passions of their patrons.

The game of mirror imaging between the observer and the scene observed continued with refined play of light and shade, whereby facades became "paintings of paintings", depictions of two worlds – one interior, the other exterior, one imagined and the other real.

At times, this hyperrealism culminated in cultured references to classic architecture which forgot the city and its limitations, overcoming physical restrictions to place the mansion in a stimulating, timeless setting.

It was precisely the ambiguity between reality and function that stimulated interest in colour. When reality shatters into infinite facets, the simple effects achieved by different colours avoid isolating the building from its actual context – be it town or country. Colour also helps define hierarchical roles and even characterises roles. Colour becomes distinction, as well as a complex equilibrium between reality and illusion, constantly torn between emotionality and imagination.

Neo-Classical reminiscences, stylised shields and ancient mouldings acquire new vigour and interest thanks to bold colours of the kind to be found only in eclectic places like Miami Beach.

Along the road between Antananarivo and Tamatave, central Madagascar, there are many villages characterised by simple architecture set off by imaginative colours.

The Emirate of Dubai boasts many mansions. The exteriors usually have few doors and windows, although perspectives are always animated by enigmatic patterns.

Kleiner Castle, Berg, Switzerland. The rather plain facade is finished with stuccowork with dark grey stripes. Even the coat of arms is colourfully painted.

Below: the entrance to this mansion in Trujillo is enhanced by trompe-l'oeil tympanums, niches and statues.

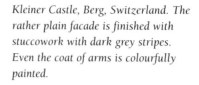

Above: trompe-l'oeil again, in the Villa dei Papiri, Ercolano, rebuilt in Malibu, California (now the Getty Museum).

Side: a vivid facade in the historic centre of Maracaibo, Venezuela.

Bas-reliefs

THE TERM "bas-relief" generally indicates a sculpted artefact in which the carved stand out only slightly from the background. The differences as regards medium- and relief lies entirely in the depth the artist gives to the scene, i.e. how many figures are r out of the main setting. Materials are generally marble, stone, wood and metals, especi bronze.

This artistic technique was already known to the Egyptians. Their attempts to achieve perspective and depth were empirical and produced by hollowing out the surface of the material to create niches. Assyrian and Babylonian art also employed the so-called flat relief technique derived from the Egyptian style. Yet the best examples, combining both technique and artistic quality, date from the Cretan-Aegean and Greek ages, the latter achieving admirable quality as well as diversifying techniques and materials, even to the extent of producing medals and metal medallions in bas-relief.

Etruscan and Roman art were inspired by both the technique and subject matter of the Greek world. The invention of the drill encouraged interesting pictorial effects and greater decorative fantasy. As a result, the use of many different colours – utilising different kinds of marble and by painting the backgrounds – fell out of favour. Christian art continued the Roman tradition, especially in the decoration of sarcophagi; bas-reliefs in Byzantine art became increasingly ornamental.

Stone bas-reliefs returned with Romanesque architecture to the point of becoming a characteristic element. The scenes are bare and symmetrical, the figures generally stand on the ground or are supported by an outline shape. Romanesque artists avoided overlapping figures and, if obliged to create them by the subject, they are superbly blended over the surface planes without protruding excessively. In the Christian East in the early Middle Ages, especially in Coptic art, fretwork carvings were also very common. During the Gothic period, bas-reliefs survived alongside high-reliefs, while gaining in simplicity and naturalness. The new style emerged in France and soon spread throughout the West. In these works, lines of perspective are shorter, the landscape more realistic and there are the first moves towards a

Above: sublime and imaginative geometrical and floral forms, simple volutes: every culture has bas-reliefs.

Following page: painted entirely in green and gold, this bas-relief decorates a facade in Chiang Mai, Thailand.

8

9

10

11

12

28

29

30

1

6

2

figures

high-

aised

lly

5

3

4

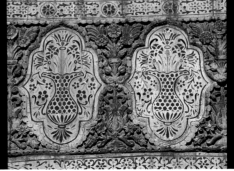

24

25

26

27

23

22

18

19

20

21

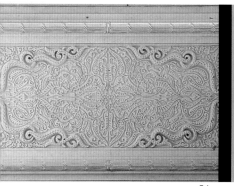

36

37

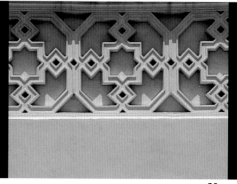

38

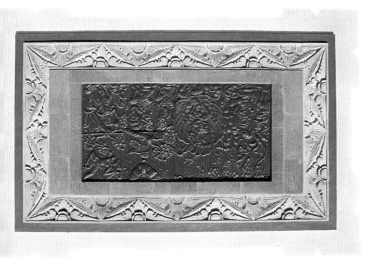

14

17

16

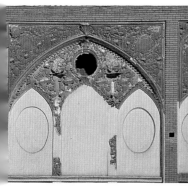

32

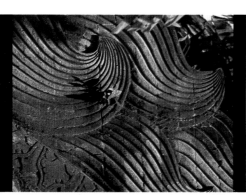

33

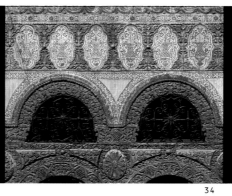

34

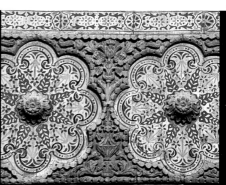

35

more pictorial style. It was a time of transition: with the rediscovery of the rules of perspective in the Renaissance, bas-reliefs enjoyed renewed popularity, based on the laws of optics and relationships with painting.

It was the period of the so-called pictorial bas-relief; marble was still the preferred material, joined by terracotta, stucco – extremely malleable but not as durable – and bronze. Bas-reliefs came to decorate frontons, barriers and wainscots. Wherever there was free space, there was room to decorate a void. Bas-reliefs were even immensely successful in theatrical stagings: the frons scenae of the Olympic Theatre in Vicenza is a major example. With the advent of Neo-Classicism, certain art critics condemned bas-reliefs as being contrary to the fundamental character of sculpture. Despite this, in the West and the colonies – finance permitting – the tympanums of new mansions were decorated with elaborate scenes, epic tales of the recent deeds of the owners and even vague echoes of the mother country.

Bas-reliefs can be divided into three main categories: figurative, geometrical and floral. Generally speaking, there is no clear line of demarcation between one style and another; different forms are often mixed in an attempt to achieve a richer and more elaborate effect. In outline, figurative bas-reliefs are especially characteristic of Western artistic traditions. In the Islamic world, on the other hand, since the depiction of living beings is discouraged, calligraphic art is more widespread, reproduced even in bas-reliefs infinitely and repeatedly engraved with proverbs, auguries and verses from the Koran. Geometrical bas-reliefs are also largely associated with Islamic art, always inspired by abstract themes. The basic form underlying Islamic decoration is the circle, where the radius acts as the basis for developing all other geometrical forms, giving rise to infinite, endless polygons and ceaseless geometrical patterns intended to communicate the uniqueness of God and His omnipresence. Mogul art, developed in India in the XVI-XVII centuries, emphasised vegetal motifs. The most frequent vegetal elements in Greek and Roman art are palm leaves (symbolising victory and honour), acanthus, laurel (also an emblem of glory and triumph) and oak; the most common floral motif is the rose.

Mosaics, stuccowork and sponges

Mosaics are a particular kind of decoration for floors and walls made up of multi-coloured, more or less regular pieces. Pebble stone work resembles mosaics but the pebbles are larger, honed and arranged to create various patterns. Pebbles were initially used for mosaic-work but were later replaced by hard stones, marbles, shells, glass paste, terracotta, mother of pearl and enamels. It is a very ancient and widespread art and related techniques have changed little over the centuries. In the East, during the Middle Ages, mosaics comprising "tesserae" (small tiles) in marble and stone were common. Held in high regard in the Byzantine age, mosaics became extremely popular, even in Islamic art, to decorate floors and inside walls. Mosaics were introduced into villa architecture during the Mannerist period.

Two views of a fountain in a courtyard in Rabat, Morocco. A large marble basin collects the water flowing from two brass spouts placed in the middle of a multi-coloured, geometrically complex mosaic. The tiny tiles are enamelled ceramics.

An inlay of stone and marble stands over one of the entrances to the residence set into the Citadel of Aleppo, Syria,

An elegant pebble-stone decoration welcomes visitors to the Pawerscourt Gardens at Ennisberry, Ireland. The pebbles come from a nearby river.

A floor in Damascus where four kinds of marble alternate to create the decoration. The geometry is formed by overlapping two squares.

Below, right: a reconstruction in Malibu, California for the Getty Museum of a Ninfeo from Villa dei Papiri in Ercolano, Italy.

The garden on Isola Bella, Stresa, Lake Maggiore, Italy, has several niches superbly decorated with pebble mosaics. The pebbles were carefully selected in relation to their shape, size and colour to form an elaborate design on a black background.

Below, left: a ceiling in the entrance patio of the Badal Mahal, a noble mansion in Jaisalmer, Rajastan, The decoration is the result of patient inlay work using local stone.

Right: a wall in the Guell Park, Barcelona, made up of tiles that are, in turn, composed of small ceramic pieces.

They were generally used to decorate architectural structures annexed to the main residence such as grottoes, niches, staircases and fountains. They were so-called "rustic" mosaics – the heirs to classic decorations – which even included imitations of rocks made by pouring liquid limestone and leaving it to set. These elements are also known as "sponges" after the porous form seen once the limestone hardened. The basic material is mortar, arranged in various layers and highlighted by different shades of the same colour. These artefacts emphasise an image of Nature dominated by disorder and chaos, where true and artificial nature blend, where limestone mouldings disguise the sharp edges and frameworks of architecture.

Stuccowork is less emblematic but nevertheless highly practical: stucco is prepared from an amalgam of lime, marble powder, sand and casein. It has been used since Antiquity to provide uniform coverage of large surface areas or to finish off variously carved and sculptured items, which

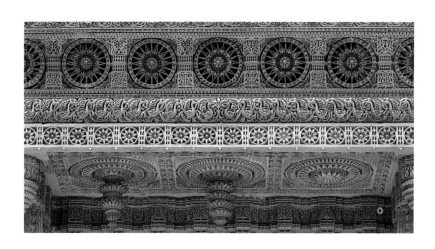

were then painted. In classical Greece, stucco was used to face columns and trabeations to imitate marble. The Romans used stucco to plaster walls using special spatulas or even the fingers, while friezes and rosettes were made using moulds and dies. Byzantine stuccowork is dense and well-defined, and often imitates inlays of precious and extremely expensive materials (frequently also involving the use of glass paste).

During the Renaissance, stucco re-emerged – in combination with other elements – in "graffiti" decorations. The layers of cement and stucco applied in two or more colours to the exteriors of buildings were decorated from cartoons using the "pouncing" method. Special spatulas were used to remove portions of the final surface: the underlying colour thus outlined the design. In the Rococo period during the 1600s-1700s, stucco was also used for interior decorations to achieve an imitation marble effect. Stucco was equally important in all Islamic art. The climate of the Near and Middle East, North Africa and Spain is ideal for the conservation of this material, which is rarely used in wet, tropical and monsoon climates. The lack of good stone and good lumber made stucco the best solution for creating the elaborate, multi-coloured decorations typical of Islamic art. This encouraged the use of decorative wall panels, with broken lines and tangent circles merging to create cloverleaf and concentric lozenge motifs. The Alhambra in Granada, Spain, and Isfahan in Shiraz, Persia, are marvellous examples; sandstone bricks were used for building and thus the walls had to be faced with a ductile material – which proved an ideal support for such decoration.

Mosaics and stucco, as well as sponge-work, shells, pebbles, inlays and a whole range of other decorative techniques, are thus used to decorate plain walls. The materials may not be precious but the effects certainly are, perhaps to show that it is always better to "appear" than to "be", at least when "visual tricks" become art.

A large niche, enclosed within an ogival arch, in a courtyard in Isfahan, Iran. All the masonry surfaces are decorated with inlays of multi-coloured stone and ceramic, set into a blue background.

A medallion in Guell Park, Barcelona. The individual pieces of the mosaic are ceramic and even cover the emblem in the centre.

Right: an austere decoration of a facade in Sana'a, Yemen, involving different stone materials.

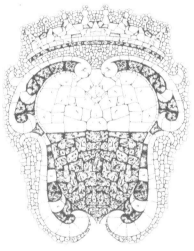

A mosaic of a noble coat of arms placed on the main facade of the Giugni Palace, in the heart of Florence.

Majolica and azulejos

It is not always easy to distinguish between mosaics and geometrically decorated majolica. This wall facing is made up of enamelled ceramic tiles (in a mansion in Sikandra, India). Even the ogival arch is itself faced with ceramics.

Majolica is a particular kind of ceramic, like terracotta and porcelain. In fact, the term "ceramic" originates from a Greek word describing the clay paste used to make this material. Majolica – a vitreous, painted ceramic – apparently takes its name from the island of Mallorca, where it was once thought to have originated. It spread in the 1300s and enjoyed its golden age in the XVI century: the main production areas in Europe were Faenza (Italy), Delft (Holland) and Antwerp (Belgium).

Ceramic art is extremely ancient and was already known to the Greeks, who used the technique, in particular, for jars and vases – objects intended to be used rather than be decorative or artistic artefacts. Yet enamelled ceramic tiles used to decorate walls and floors are just as old and common, although cultural references and production techniques differed from civilisation to civilisation.

In the Islamic east, for example, where majolica was manufactured on a large scale, the enamelling technique was improved through contact with Chinese craftsmen skilled in porcelain, whose work travelled the Silk Route as far as artistic centres in Persia, Syria and Mesopotamia. The best examples of Islamic tiles are thus perhaps Persian and Ottoman. From a manufacturing point of view, these products are distinguished by the so-called "metal lustre", a delicate, iridescent patina achieved by annealing vitreous ceramics (after painting) in an oxygen-free atmosphere.

Production of enamelled and painted terracotta tiles remained a small-scale, repetitive process in the workshops of many small craftsman. Illustrious exceptions include the Della Robbia family in Florence, especially Luca, who – in the mid-1500s – perfected the production technique for vitreous bas-relief sculptures. Figurative elegance, expressiveness and detailed attention to painting made the Della Robbia famous throughout Renaissance Europe.

Exchanges between artists at the courts of Europe developed with alliances and declined when war broke out. These movements saw majolica spread throughout France, thanks particularly to Italian artists invited there by Caterina de' Medici. Ceramic workers from Faenza made a major contribution in Holland, where they were welcomed into the

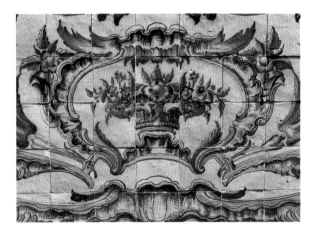

Three different kinds of vitreous terracotta: floral motifs in Isfahan; azulejos in Villa Berardo, Madeira (evidently of Portuguese inspiration); the majolica of the Patio de los Arrayanes, Alhambra, Granada.

111

This majolica in the Norman Palace, Palermo, with volutes and bands, is clearly inspired by Arab art.

Below: a figurative azulejo in the Hacienda Chillo Jijon, Ecuador, showing a knight in armour, clearly derives from a Spanish background.

This majolica composition on the walls around the Villa Gaslini, Genoa, Italy, is a rare example of application on a large scale.

Side: a geometrical azulejo with the traditional Portuguese background in a garden in Madeira.

The main gate to the Villa Berardo near Fuchal, Madeira, includes even figurative azulejos.

corporations of painters – thus enjoying the status of artists – while in Spain, especially in Seville, their reception was lukewarm. It is no coincidence that the experience of the *mudejar* artists inspired by Hispanic-Moorish culture was much closer to the cultural climate of the Iberian peninsula. The workshops in Seville exported the vitreous ceramic production technique to Portugal. The most likely date for this event was the visit to Spain by King Emanuel I in 1498. After visiting the Andalusa, the King decided to decorate his residence in Sintra in the same style. Enamelled tiles were not entirely unknown in Portugal, but were mainly used for floors and to decorate fountains. However, they are ideal for warm climates, since they reflect the rays of the sun.

The phenomenon of *azulejaria* in Portugal, monopolising the decoration of buildings and gardens from the 1400s to the present-day, is rather curious, especially in view of the fact that Spanish, Italian and Dutch production was far superior for many years. The so-called *azulejos* created stories and evocations, amplifying an exuberant decorative imagination by depicting religious, mythological and historical themes that even developed into full-scale examples of trompe-l'oeil.

There were many periods. The white and blue age, influenced by Dutch production, lasted through to the end of the 1600s and is especially characterised by the inspiration taken from Flemish engravings. Floral subjects included lilies, tulips, roses, camellias and passion-flowers. From the 1700s, thanks in particular to income from the gold and diamond mines in Brazil, *azulejaria* in Portugal achieved its greatest splendour: large cornices, scrolls, trompe-l'oeil and later, in the Rococo period, even a return to multi-coloured articles. The art declined in the 1800s but has re-emerged in contemporary output.

Whatever the manufacturing technique, these tiles are an important, versatile and expressive decorative element still in great demand and widely appreciated.

A wall around a garden in Algiers. The plastered masonry is faced with geometrical majolica tiles.

Side: a green ceramic decorative motif; a mould was used to create bas-reliefs with geometrical patterns.

Majolica and azulejos

The term azulejo *derives from the Arab word* azzeli *("flat, smooth stone") and was originally used to describe the Roman-Byzantine mosaics found throughout the Near East and North Africa. It was from these areas, following Muslim invasions, that the technique was taken to the Iberian Peninsula by Arab artists specialising in coloured tiles. They settled mainly in Malaga, Seville and Valencia, thereby creating local traditions of azulejo in those places. The new technique – albeit already known in Ancient Egypt, Mesopotamia and the Near East – soon spread through the conquered lands. From the 1500s, azulejos in Portugal became increasingly important, to the extent of becoming one of the most significant forms of art in the country. It is not clear how this occurred, since Portugal was practically isolated from the rest of the world during the Spanish occupation (1580-1640). Perhaps it was due to the continuation of Arab traditions (at the time more diluted in cosmopolitan Spain) and ideal climatic conditions (frost is the worst enemy of azulejos and*

majolica, possibly combined with a rather archaic lifestyle, where women rarely ventured out of their homes and thus needed enclosed but elegant and pleasant places where they could pass most of the day. All this influenced the design of villas and palaces, which consequently included porticoes, patios and walled gardens where azulejo art was the ideal decorative complement. Three preparation techniques were developed: alicantados involved monochromatic tiles with various geometrical forms and patterns inspired by mosaics. This was a rather costly method involving laborious installation work, so it was

not particularly popular. The corda seca technique, on the other hand, involved engraving the outlines of the decorative pattern directly on the uncured clay tile. These grooves were then filled with a mixture of manganese oxide and flax oil, which, once baked, turned black. These outlines prevented the other colours applied to the tile from merging during the baking process. Aresta or cucenca techniques involved a negative model which was pressed against the surface of the tile before it was baked. The relief and recessed outlines thus formed marked off the colour zones without leaving black bordering lines. It was the most economic

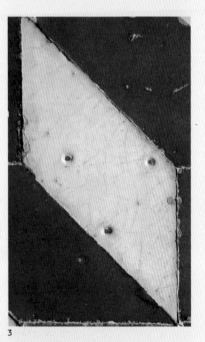

method and even if the final result was not always perfect, it was nevertheless ideal for large-scale production. The materials employed were blends of clay, which had to be homogeneous and rich in silica; they were baked prior to colouring, using pastes containing pigments obtained from various metal oxides: cobalt (blue), copper (green), manganese (brown), iron (yellow) and tin (white). These pastes were arranged on a base of lead oxide and then baked. A more shiny result was achieved by applying a layer of silver and copper alloy over this enamel and then baking/curing for a third time.

The most common form, from the 1500s onwards, was square. Unlike majolica, azulejo has a pattern produced by a mould or die or – in more elaborate instances – by a mosaic made up of many small tiles. Techniques resembling fresco painting and majolica were used only in more important and figurative works. This involved the preparation of a white enamel (tin oxide) applied to the "biscuit" (the uncured tile), transferring a pattern using stencils and charcoal dust and, finally, hand-painting. Subsequent oven-curing made the design and it's colouring entirely permanent. This intricate technique, affordable only to wealthier patrons, is exemplified by many superb creations.

1. The complex motif in this wall decoration in Madeira comprises many tiles each having a different pattern.

2. Hand-painting of vitreous tiles.

3. The holes made in the support brackets to cure a tile: Sintra Palace, Portugal.

4. Application of the vitreous agglomerate to the "biscuit".

5. A two-colour tile.

6. The clay cut to shape is left to dry for 2-5 months.

7. A two-colour figurative composition.

8. An ancient example of the Seville school.

Medallions, festoons and garlands

Medallions are carved or painted figures inserted in an oval or round cornice. In residential architecture, medallions were decorative motifs used – especially during the early Renaissance – to embellish facades. The most common were vitreous terracotta decorated with elegant and various colours. These colours were produced from the madder shrub, particularly common in Asia Minor and certain parts of the Mediterranean, whose root extracts provided a deep red powder extensively used for time immemorial to prepare dyes. At various later stages, the decorative potential of medallions was revived, especially in facades and interiors, often in association with festoons.

Festoons are a decorative motif comprising flowers and fruit linked by a ribbon, which may or may not be supported at the two extremities by rosettes. The word derives from "festa", in

An elaborate stucco rosette in a mansion in Maracaibo. In the early 1900s, with the petroleum boom, these decorations were in great demand, so much so that they were often made using moulds rather than modelling them on-site.

Right: a fronton inserted in a curved tympanum in the facade of Templeton House, Long Island, New York State.

Opposite page, top: a decorative element inspired by medallions, characterised by sharp colour contrast. Side: a festoon inserted between the scrolls of an Ionic capital (early 1700s).

Opposite page, bottom: a simple medallion in Maracaibo. The characteristic decorative effect is accentuated by the colour contrast.

Left: a two-colour medallion on a facade in Maracaibo. They are chalk elements, often made using moulds.

Right: a capital embraced by a festoon in a Roman palace (late-1700s).

turn deriving from the Latin *fanum* ("holy place"), thus indicating the origins of this decorative element. Festoons (real garlands or stone ones, carvings or stuccowork) once embellished temples during festivals and rituals, later appearing in temple friezes decorated with sacrificial instruments, hanging between the skulls of sacrificed animals.

Festoons were also offered for the dead, perhaps symbolising the victory of life over the after-world or to honour earthly deeds. Festoons were used as a compositional, rather than an isolated, element, alternating with medallions or garlands. They lost their religious significance during the Renaissance to become simple decorations set off by tympanums, shields and storey markers. Skulls were largely replaced by masques, cherubs, lion heads and blazons.

Circular festoons are known as garlands and were originally crowns of leaves, symbolising honour, made with branches of laurel, oak, olive or other plants held together by a ribbon. A laurel crown was awarded to the winner of the ancient games held in Delphos, Greece, in honour of Apollo, while an olive garland went to the winner of the Olympic Games. Victorious Roman generals and emperors were granted crowns of laurel or oak, which were also depicted in triumphal arches, grasped by "Winged Victory". The natural elements included in medallions, festoons and garlands were particularly significant: in classic art, they were associated with a god or magical and holy powers.

In the Middle Ages and the Renaissance, this pagan animism

Opposite page, bottom: a floral festoon in Warsaw and a festoon with leaves and pomegranates in the main hall of Villa Strozzi, Begozzo, near Mantua, Italy.

Below: a simple festoon in Singapore, highlighted by a colourful background.

Right: a motif developed from the medallion in a facade in Coro, Venezuela.

Bottom: a full-bodied festoon focusing on a pomegranate – a symbol of prosperity – in the main hall of Villa Strozzi, Begozzo, near Mantua, Italy.

was interpreted in the symbols of saints, epic deeds and even heraldry. Symbolism became rather complex: the grape vine was associated with Bacchus, the god of fertility and wine, and the pomegranate, too, with fertility. The lily symbolised purity, while the poppy, given its soporific effects, was related to Hypnos, the Greek god of sleep, and Morpheus, the god of dreams.

Heraldic shields

The coats of arms of noble families decorate villas and mansions with an unmistakable mark of ownership. Testimony of a courtly past, shields today not only decorate but also narrate the history of the residence – such as changes in ownership – and, for the elite few, even take the place of visiting cards. In the Middle Ages, shields – the Greek word indicated the crown of laurel embellishing images of their forefathers – were an essential tool of war. The decorations of these shields later became hereditary and served the practical purpose of identifying combatants or knights competing in tourneys. After 1200, the most powerful families marked all their weapons with these insignia and, a century later, the first examples began to appear on castles and palaces. It is no coincidence that the term "heraldry" derives from "herald", the person who carried invitations to outsiders during festivals and ensured observance of the rules during tourneys. Heralds later became shield bearers, whose task it was to check the arms and armour of knights competing in tournaments and, especially, to ensure that the insignia on their shields matched the laws of heraldry.

The Middle Ages saw the greatest inventive fervour in this field, although the Renaissance also saw the introduction of various accessories intended to distinguish between different shields following the proliferation of coats of arms. From the 1500s, with the ascent of Charles VIII, coats of arms came to include the deeds and mottoes of noble families. Intricate developments in design and the search for new symbols and combinations continued until the French Revolution, when heraldry suffered a harsh blow, since shields were viewed as symbols of tyranny. Later, Napoleon was excessively generous with blazons and investitures. Shields – or coats of arms - are the major and most common form of such insignia, since they were the main element in a knight's armour. They are generally divided into several fields, which may be vertical, horizontal or diagonal, each with their own names: partitioned, truncated, cut and so forth. The embellishments generally placed above or around the shield vary enormously: there may be a helmet on top, replaced for prelates by the papal tiara or the cardinal's hat. Shields – generally carved in stone, more rarely in marble and almost never in iron – are generally (especially for the more ancient) bas-reliefs set into walls.

The shield in painted wrought iron standing over the main gate to Glorup Castle, Svendborg, Denmark.

Top right: a wooden coat of arms on Good Hope Great House, Jamaica. The wood inlay is Anglo-Saxon in style.

Opposite page: a stone shield walled into the façade of Castelpuig, Gurb, near Barcelona.

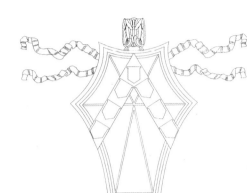

Side: the shield in pietra serena on the main gate to the Ginori Palace in Florence.

Below: the marble shield surmounted by an iron crown on the facade of the Villa Duchessa di Galliera in Genoa.

An inside wall in the Sultan's Palace, Yogyakarta, has this shield of the Sultan in gilt and lacquered wood.

Side: a simple shield, carved directly into a block of stone in Merida, Venezuela.

Bottom: the supreme divinity of Zoroastrism, Ahura Mazda (Shiraz, Iran).

From the Renaissance onwards, even three-dimensional shields were developed, with many concave and convex surfaces and even many colours, which improved visibility and created a new spatial hierarchy. They were usually secured to walls with iron brackets to crown facades and balusters; at times, they were placed in frontons or the keystones over entrances and gates. Colonial heraldry wrote its own history. Colonists in the new territories found a largely virgin land, lacking in facilities, history and traditions. Social fabric and government apparatus had to be developed from scratch, taking inspiration from the mother country. New architectural styles were also accompanied by "operetta" heraldry, colourful and picturesque, decorated with pineapples and bananas where pure white lilies and solemn crowns once held sway. Stone and marble were replaced by less expensive wood and even stuccowork. Few of these coats of arms represented true nobility but the important thing was, above all else, self-celebration.

Today, heraldry refers to a figurative language based on mythological, allegorical and natural images evoking ancient origins, privileges and family ties. Like a forgotten language, it arouses a sense of mystery and curiosity, a somewhat snobbish component of the history of villas, as well as our roots and traditions.

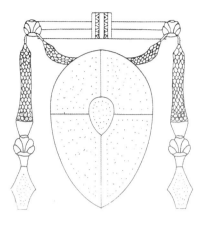

Left: the 1400s shield on the facade of Schifanoia Palace, Ferrara.

Below: the Medici emblem in Carrara white marble surmounted by a crown, positioned over the entrance to Villa la Petraia, on a hillside outside Florence.

Below: the shield of the Sultan of Brunei, on the wall around the Embassy in Kuala Lumpur.

Bottom right: two shields paired on a wall inside the Sacred Wood of Bomarzo, commissioned by Prince Orsini. They are engraved in white plaster with fields in red.

Masques

This monstrous gate by Zuccari in Rome is one of the most impressive masques of Italian Mannerism.

An anthropomorphic masque (1600s) acts as the spout for a fountain in Villa La Pietra just outside Florence.

Masques are faces in various materials and styles used to impart different features – human, diabolical or animal – to the wearer and to express a different personality. The most ancient masques were funerary, when it was the custom to cover the faces of the dead. This custom took its origins from the belief in magic common to many peoples, and the belief that life would only continue after death if the head remained intact. Masques were thus fitted, not least to protect the dead against malign demons, but also in an attempt to preserve the appearance of the person. The burial masques of ancient Egypt are particularly impressive. The materials used had to withstand humidity and to be easily worked as well as strong. Gold and silver were therefore widely used for this purpose – especially gold, which was believed to possess magical powers. In Imperial Rome, less precious materials were also used, such as bronze and even papier-mâché, chalk, clay, terracotta and wax. Masques were also used in religious ceremonies and propitiatory rites. Masques not only disguised their wearers but also transformed their essence. People ceased to be particular individuals for a moment and took on a new identity: animal or demi-god, satyr or demon.

It was also believed that masques possessed apotropaic properties, so that depicting the ambivalent characters of demons, involving grotesque outlines, would ensure that these natural spirits could be dominated and favourably influenced. When, with the passing of time, this fear of demons gradually abated, so did the powers attributed to them. Nevertheless, the pleasure of costume and role-playing remained and continued for centuries in the world of theatre. In Athens, following the introduction of three new kinds of play – tragedies, comedies and satires – the profane and playful use of masques became widespread. They were very effective for identifying the various characters, since the stylised facial features were clearly visible even to the most distant spectators and also immediately communicated emotions and states of mind. For Greek actors, the masque never lost its holy attributes. The actor merged with the character: he did not play Dionysus – he WAS Dionysus.

The nature of these two kinds of masque – holy and profane – blended in the 1500s in the large masks used for essentially decorative purposes. These had human or animal faces in a

Another 1600s masque in white marble in the gardens of Villa La Pietra, near Florence, The mouth spouts water.

The main gate of Villa Comboni, Toscolano, near Brescia, Italy, has a finely carved masque in the keystone.

grotesque or caricature style and were used as, among other things, fountain spouts, keystones or embrasures. The best-known and most interesting examples date from the late Mannerist period, when the form became more independent and much larger. In this period, the masques/masks and monstrous figures included in tympanums and embrasures seem to be spontaneously emerging from the wall or stone, like Michelangelo's "Prisoners" desperately seeking freedom. Animal masques frequently appeared in the scrolls and noble coats of arms in the 1500s and 1600s. The Church never approved of this proliferation of satyrs and monsters and, especially during the Counter Reformation, they were openly banned from religious buildings since "inappropriate anywhere, they are intolerable in Churches", as Cardinal Paleotti wrote in 1582; putto and cherubs were far more preferable.

Caricature developed in the 1600-1700s, but was rarely used to decorate buildings and was only in part similar to masques. While masques exchanged human and animal lineaments, caricature was much more realistic and its style fresher and more innovative. The magical and evocative role of masques, in any case, was long forgotten.

Opposite page, top left: two masques used in Greek theatre. Generally in terracotta, they served to amplify the facial expressions of actors so that even distracted spectators could understand them.

Opposite page, top right: an animalesque masque representing a divinity, carved in stone on a pyramid in Mexico.

Opposite page, bottom: anthropomorphic representation in Water Castle, Yogyakarta, Java.

Top left: a face set into volutes in a bas-relief carving.

Top right: a grotesque face in the Giusti Gardens, Verona, Italy. The interior can be visited and the mouth was used as a viewpoint.

Bottom left: a mask at the side of the gate of Villa Palagonia in Bagheria, near Palermo. Night-time visitors put out their torch flames in its mouth.

Bottom right: an elegant face that was once the base impost for a step, now lost, in the courtyard of an ancient palace in Malta.

Hanging gardens

The impressive facade of an 1800s villa in Lonigo, near Vicenza, Italy. The dense ivy disguises the Neo-Classic style of the villa.

The Romantic park of Muskau, Germany, has various buildings – some deliberately resembling ruins, others such as this one surmounted by tall gables.

In the 1700s, gardens became the main setting for the social rituals of the nobility. They resembled stages, with the trees and tall plants representing buildings. The great ferment in the 1700s in the world of theatrical stage design, especially the "corner-pieces" of Ferdinando Gali Bibiena, helped break down more linear approaches by creating multi-directional lines of perspective where the central role of Man – the lynch-pin of Renaissance culture – became less important.

Having exhausted the experimental scope of dimensional variables, patrons and designers laid the basis for a radical escape from everything "constructed". The demise of the geometrical garden was close at hand: fountains and ornamental lakes grew larger, avenues became winding and the English style garden became increasingly popular.

The infinite variations of geometry seemed all but played out and, as the Humanist force which had driven these developments lost its thrust, Man "relaxed", rediscovering "natural" Nature – which he no longer sought to tame but only to make softer, more amenable and in harmony with the idyllic image that Romantic painting was then outlining.

Nature was thus rediscovered and re-assessed in all its randomness and when it was not quite random enough, it was given a helping hand. The new pergolas brought the garden closer to the villa and at times this structure even continued along the walls of the building. Preference was given to climbing plants, since they require little attention; originally, the grape-vine predominated, then other plants, such as honeysuckle, wisteria, ivy and roses, became popular: Experience gained in England guided and inspired the development of gardens throughout Europe in the XIX century.

England had never entirely accepted the grandiose and intransigent classicism of the "French" garden. The Englishman's love of the landscape required greater harmony – living within rather than apart from Nature, which was therefore neither tamed nor re-modelled.

The terraces of the "Italian" garden were abolished, as were the stairways built to link them. The landscape became undulating and without abrupt interruptions, sharp outlines or steep green "walls". Symmetry disappeared; borders and paths became more twisted to avoid right angles; patios were replaced by open lawns, which often came right up to the villa. Fountains

Above: Villa Allegri at Grezzana, Verona, Italy, dates from the 1600s but retains traces of an earlier, Mediaeval building, such as this turret.

Side: an un-used side entrance to Lednice Palace, Slovakia, near the border with Austria.

Evergreen climbing plants and colourful flowers alternate in decorating the facade of a villa on Isola Madre, Stresa, Lake Maggiore, Italy.

St. Emilion, Bordeaux region, is home to the Villa Ausone. One of the annexes is practically submerged by vegetation.

also disappeared, although water still played an important role, but now as placid streams and still pools. Ornamentation was replaced by harmonious "paintings" with trees, lawns, streams, lakes and tiny islands and bridges. Obviously, there was no room for mazes or landscape gardening.

At the same time, greenhouses became important, designed to house full-scale protected gardens, so that plants which would not have survived outside could be grown.

An important contribution to the definition of the Romantic garden was made by the architect Giovanni Battista Piranesi, whose engravings of the ruins of classic Rome were widely published and inspired the fashion for archaeological and architectural ruins. Thanks to his work, Romantic parks were embellished with obelisks, urns, inscriptions, benches, sarcophagus, statues and busts. The new ruins were shown in a state of utter, unliveable and final deterioration, testimony to the definitive demise of the culture they represented as well as being involuntary harbingers of an imminent new decline. The advent of the Industrial Revolution swept away the foundations on which villa life was based. There were many new patrons but they did not enjoy unlimited financial resources, and land, especially in towns, was increasingly more expensive. Thus, even the garden fell into decline and underwent many formal and substantial compromises merely to survive.

One of these "compromises" was the hanging or vertical garden. Bare walls were "decorated" with climbing plants, thereby disguising the underlying architecture. Though this a compromise, it nevertheless created an often delightful link between Nature and buildings – with decorative outcomes that bear comparison with stone and other embellishments.

Long Island, New York, is dotted with admirable villas built in the early 1900s, such as Westbury Villa, where the large garden continues on the facade.

The facade of the cellars of the Margaux Estate, Bordeaux, is completely disguised by climbing plants.

Wrought iron

This elegant bracket in wrought iron graces the wall of a villa in Spanish Town, the ancient capital of Jamaica.

Top right: a wind vane crowned with a fish in the Neo-Gothic style.

IRON is a grey-blue, ductile and malleable metal, it is very strong, plentiful in nature and relatively inexpensive. The first product made from this ore was cast iron, a fragile, rigid compound used to make very basic artefacts. Later, cast iron was poured to make ingots or bars, which were then re-heated; this characteristically red-white material was then hammered with large mauls and became much harder. Craftsmen use this raw material in the form or square or flat bars, round rods or even in sheets.

The Etruscans already knew of iron and worked with it, while the Romans discovered how to forge bars to produce tools. However, the first artefacts in wrought iron used for artistic purposes date from the XI century. These include doors for churches and weather vanes in the form of cockerels, which were used to crown many buildings. From the 1200s, central Europe and especially the Ile de France saw the introduction of moulds, which made it possible to reproduce even the smallest details on a large scale. This technique, combined with wrought iron hammering, was widely employed for large works and, once the noble features of the material were recognised, even architects began to explore and develop the new expressive possibilities it offered.

In the Neo-Classic period, wrought iron went out of fashion, partly because of the competition from cast iron, but it became popular again at the end of the 1800s, achieving its "golden age" in the Liberty period. By then the artistic potential of the metal was fully exploited and it was accepted as a good substitute for bronze.

When combined with other elements and no more than 1.7% of carbon, iron becomes steel. Depending on the content of carbon, steels are said to be extra-mild, mild, semi-hard, hard and extra-hard. There are four main processing techniques: engraving, damask-work, die-casting and wrought hammering (the first two are generally used for small artefacts).

Engraving is especially used for locks, where several sheets of metal are overlapped but kept apart by small pins. Each sheet is cold-engraved to produce a pattern which allows underlying patterns to be seen. In the 1500s in Nuremberg, a well-known metalworking centre, locks were engraved directly into the solid metal, which was then decorated using burins and other gravers.

Left: a ring for tying up horses and a torch holder on the roughly finished facade of the Medici Riccardi Palace, Florence.

Top: wrought iron is used to striking effect in Casa Milá, Barcelona, designed by Catalan architect Antoni Guadì.

The railing dating from the second half of the 1800s in Powerscourt Villa, Enniskerry, Ireland.

A grating in wrought iron with delightful scroll patterns.

A Neo-Gothic wall lamp in Jerusalem.

A decorative element in wrought iron standing on a column in a courtyard in Damascus.

Damask-work is a decorative technique involving inlays of several metals (usually gold and silver). False damask-work involves roughening the surface of the base metal, using a rasp, so that the precious metal, in the form of threads or leaf, holds better when hammered over the base. In contrast, true damask-work involves cutting a groove in the base metal and placing the threads or leaf inside and these are then hammered. At times, this system is imitated by braze-welding a pre-prepared decorative pattern over the artefact being processed. Die-casting was already known at the end of the 1300s, but it was only in the Renaissance that objects produced in this manner came to be used for artistic purposes, notwithstanding their mass-produced nature. Many gates, railings and balusters were made using this method. The individual components were assembled using rivets, welding (at about 950°C) or inter-locking fittings.

Wrought iron work produces unique articles that are always different because of the manual skills the process entails. The material is worked by hammering it on an anvil when cold or molten, depending on the processing required, and great care has to be taken over the power of each blow: just slightly too much force may cause cracks which are extremely difficult to eliminate.

Even today, master wrought iron craftsmen are still in great demand. Their clients evidently seek status symbols and appreciate the inventive skill of these specialist craftsmen in combining ancient traditions with modern requirements.

Unusually, the castle of San Martino, near Bologna, Italy, has the family coat of arms in wrought iron set into a lightweight frame supported by a bird.

Bottom left: the chapel of Villa Pegazzera, Montalato Pavese, Italy, is crowned by a small bell set into a decorative emblem.

Bottom right: the 1800s wrought iron and glass roof over the gates of Kestzthely Palace, Hungary.

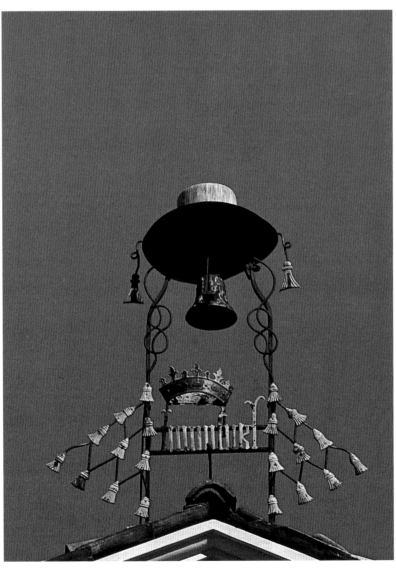

SUNDIALS

CLOCKS

ARMILLARY SPHERES

In classical Greece, there were three Hours: Eunomia ("justice"), Dice ("equity") and Irene ("peace"). The daughters of Zeus and Themis, they were not only the guardians of the gates of Olympus but were also responsible for the order of Nature and the alternation of the seasons. They were prestigious and powerful figures whose tasks held sway over many important states of human life. "The ethereal gates were guarded by the Hours, who presided over the great heavens and Olympus itself, opening and closing the dense cloud which hides the home of the Gods" (Illiad , V), to which we might add "hides the end of men". The Hours were later increased to five, including Carpus and Tallus, and then to twelve.

The pagan cycles, which for so long formed the basis for measuring time, were transformed with Christianity into a linear and progressive concept. With Galileo, time became a sequence of innumerable, identical instants, while for Einstein it was not universal but related to a system, to the extent that even its measurement is relative.

"Grasping" time and measuring its passing are recurrent human themes. Since time is a subjective measurement, it requires objective instruments, i.e. tools associated with the cyclic nature of phenomena so that they can be measured. Human, natural and musical rhythms can give rise only to approximate, unscientific measurements. In different cultures, countries and periods, an infinite number of methods have been studied to measure the passing of time. The hours, their number and their duration varied enormously, even to the point of including or excluding night. Ultimately, measurement of time was based on its most evident cycle: the alternation of day and night. Sundials were the first instruments used for measuring the passage of time; it was only in much more recent times that mechanical instruments have appeared, such as wall-clocks, pocket- and wristwatches. It seems that Man will never be able to modify the action of time and so can only measure its passing, develop statistics and forecasts, and perhaps implement cosmetic changes. Today, as in the past, no one can "stop" time. Sundials and clocks on the facades of buildings merely mark its movement.

Sundials

This square sundial surrounded by a broad border is painted on a plasterwork wall in the inner courtyard of Baranow Castle, Poland.

Opposite page, top: a circular sundial standing over the cellars of the Centermerle Estates in Macau, Bordeaux.

Opposite page, bottom: partly hidden by garden foliage, this sundial embellishes a villa in Varenna, Lake Como.

Beginning with the megaliths of Stonehenge and the sophisticated measurements in China in the XIII century A.D., the measurement of time has always fascinated mankind. Early empirical methods were gradually replaced by increasing scientific rigour to define the laws by which the shadow of the sun could be used to indicate the passing of time. The Greeks learned how to make sundials from Babylon and themselves developed gnomonics on a scientific and geometrical basis to improve on earlier methods. The works of Democritus (IV century A.D.) and Ptolomey (II century A.D.) were followed by innumerable sundials of various designs, including portable versions. Various examples, revealed during excavation work in Pompeii, Ostia and the Palatine Hill in Rome, bear witness to a deep-rooted tradition in Roman times.

The use of sundials continued through the Middle Ages, although the modest requirements for precision meant that little real progress was made. With the Renaissance and the rediscovery of technical and scientific topics, Europe witnessed the spread of sundials in palaces and villas. In the Baroque age, sundials were even installed in gardens and parks, where they became decorative items. The technique was further developed, precision improved and costs were reduced, so that such instruments were accessible to ever larger numbers of people.

Sundials may be horizontal, vertical or "camera obscura" in design. The latter system was especially used in religious buidings. A small hole in the south-facing wall or the roof of the building allowed a ray of sun to penetrate inside and illuminate a section of the floor decorated with notches which made it possible to calculate time. They were functional rather than decorative devices. Obviously, the angle and diameter of the ray changed with the seasons and it was up to the skill of the designer to make sure that these dials were always legible. Horizontal or vertical sundials, on the other hand, have always been highly decorative. The horizontal version is undoubtedly one of the first such devices, used since remotest antiquity in various forms. The simplest was a vertical post, used in Egypt 4000 years ago, which latter developed into an obelisk placed in the centre of a square. The Egyptans raised many such obelisks for this purpose. Numerous portable flat or column-like

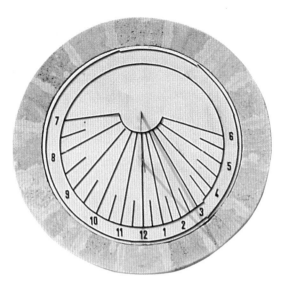

The sundial gracing the left hand tympanum of Villa Barbaro at Moser, Treviso, Italy.

The complex sundial inserted in the gables crowning the Estense Palace in Varese, Italy.
Side: dated, 1823, this sundial is painted on the facade of a villa in Briançon, France.

Bottom: this stone sundial in the Forbidden City, Peking, indicates not only the time but also many other items of information.

Opposite page: a fine example of an Italian sundial (Piuro, near Sondrio).

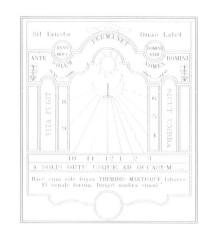

sundials were based on the same principle, and were used by merchants and trade caravans in particular. Whatever the geographical position of the horizontal sundial, time was calculated with relative ease since the device exploited the duration of sunlight to a greater extent than did vertical dials.

In truth, only vertical devices should really be called sundials, although the term is used to describe all dials fitted with a gnomon, - from the Greek "*gnomon*" (indicator) – the rod whose shadow thrown by the sun marks the local time on the dial. The art of making sundials is known as "gnomonics". The gnomon may have various shapes: the most common is the stylus, the classic metal rod set into the wall at different angles depending on the latitude and

This horizontal copper sundial, standing on a pedestal, is found by a villa in Madeira.

Below, left: the sundial of Villa Sommi Picenardi at Olgiate, near Como, Italy, is outlined by a scroll.

Below, right: this colourful sundial decorates a tympanum in Sitges, on the coastline of Catalonia.

orientation of the dial itself. The stylus has a gnomonic tip if the time of day has to be known precisely. If the dial is to provide more than one reading, a dual gnomon may be fitted. These instruments were often embellished and enriched with the addition of inscriptions or mottoes, at times obscure at others explicit, frequently embodying ancient wisdom and inspired by the inevitable passing of time and inexorable coming of death. Such inscriptions were often joined by patterns and floral elements, stars, the sun, the moon and the signs of the Zodiac. The frames around such dials were also imaginatively decorated and varied.

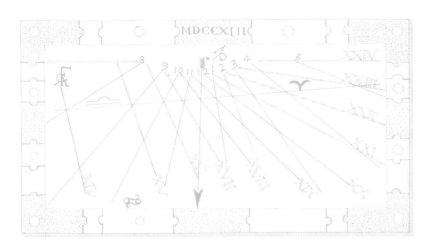

The complex 1700s sundial at the Acaja Palace, Vigone, near Turin, is engraved in a slab of stone.

Below: the centre of this sinuous tympanum in Helbrunn Palace, Salzburg, is occupied by a sundial.

Top left: a 1700s sundial on the facade of a villa at Polonghera, Cuneo, Italy.

Left, centre: a painted sundial in the courtyard of Le Nouveau Château, Oberdiessbach, Switzerland. The metal gnomon is set in the centre of a painted sun.

Side: Villa Barbaro at Moser, Treviso, Italy. The two wings are both decorated with sundials.

Above: a complex instrument for measuring time standing in the courtyard of Howard Castle, Malton, Great Britain.

Side: the austere merloned tympanum of Konopiste Castle, Czech Republic, with a simple sundial in the middle.

Clocks

Mankind has always tried to "grasp" time; even primitive man carved propitiatory signs on the walls of caves in an effort to foresee and control the future. Although the senses can perceive and evaluate various kinds of measurement, they are easily tricked by time and are totally unreliable for measuring its passing. The more time is fleeting, the more we try to define it, control it and understand its mechanisms.

Man, without instruments, can relay only on intervals between one event and another: the rhythm of music, heart-beats, the alternation of day and night, the seasons, the cycle of generations. Atomic clocks, the most sophisticated equipment currently available, measure time in relation to a frequency sample, a repetitive event of infinitely tiny duration. Despite such precision, the passing of long periods – such as years – is still calculated through astronomical observations, which are even used to "adjust" atomic instruments. An hour is 1/24th of a day and, divided into 60 minutes or 3600 seconds, accompanying our entire life-span. The astronomic hour is regulated by the passage of stars over a local meridian, although it is accepted international practice to use the time defined by time zones. Summer time, GMT, star-time, canonical time and biological time are all representations of time and its progress.

Many myths have arisen in the vain hope of understanding this fleeting medium that prevents us grasping the present, turns everything immediately into the past and, before we even realise it, turns the future into the present. Borges wrote in *Otras inquiscionas* : "time is the substance of which I am made. Time is a river which pulls me in its flow, but I am the river; it is a tiger devouring me, but I am the tiger; it is a fire which burns me, but I am the fire". Perhaps the secret is to accept its passing, go with the flow and savour the fruits of every season.

The progress from ancient sand and water clocks to mechanical instruments was long and complex. These later clocks have cogged wheels set in movement by a weight or spring controlled by a pendulum or a rocker-arm and they ensure previously unthinkable regularity and constancy.

Above: turrets have always provided an ideal home for clocks, as they are particularly visible.

Following page: a clock with gilt figures in the fronton of Stromsholm Castle in Sweden.

6

9

ANNO 1710

7

8

25

26

27

1

5

2

4

3

21

22

23

24

16

19

17

18

20

33

34

35

10

14

15

1

13

12

29

9 MAI 1872.

30

31

32

The first examples of clocks mounted on towers and facades date from the XIII century. The credit is contended between Italy and England, although it should be recognised that Humanist capitals such as Florence, Mantua, Milan, Ferrara and Bologna, with their economic and cultural progress, the foundation of the first universities and the influence of the Orient introduced by the Crusaders, represented particularly favourable and receptive environments for such developments. Churches were initially the preferred sites for clocks, yet in later times villas too welcomed this new device and clocks became increasingly common, especially on the facades of private homes.

Placing a clock on the facade of a villa has always represented a desire to control the progress of time and to appear capable of dominating the course of events. Invented in the late-XII, early XIII centuries, mechanical clocks began to appear more frequently in facades in the XVIII century, set in frontons or gables in alternation with coats of arms. Such ancient and modern timepieces still mark off the rhythms of villas. Placed in tympanums and gables, in simple frames or voluptuous stuccowork, clocks, like a coat of arms or a bust, link villas with the great themes of living and being. Today as yesterday, these instruments remind us to be "happy when you can", since tomorrow offers no certainties.

Armillary spheres

In 1363, a doctor, chemist, mathematician and astronomer from Padua – Giovanni Dondi – built a celebrated instrument that his contemporaries defined as an "astrarium". As the name suggests, it was an elaborate device that reproduced the movement of the stars. The base was a full-scale clock, while the upper part comprised a mechanism that illustrated the orbits of the sun, the moon, Mars, Mercury, Venus, Jupiter and Saturn.

The mechanical movement was operated by a spring, independently of sunlight, and was capable – among other things – of indicating the time in any kind of light. Its operating

Above: an armillary sphere of the mid-1800s (private collection). It is an English model in brass by Nathaniel Hill.

Right: an armillary sphere on a stone pedestal beside a large mansion in Los Angeles, California.

Left: the frontispiece to a 1700s treatise of astronomy by Luca Gaurico, depicting Pythagorus and Ptolomey at the sides and a complex armillary sphere in the middle.

Below: an armillary sphere in perfect condition in Amerongen Estate, Holland.

Left: this armillary sphere standing on a marble base faces the Huntington Estate in Los Angeles.

principle was mid-way between the most ancient systems – megaliths arranged in patterns on the ground – and more complex armillary spheres. The latter are astrolabe-clocks made up of the inter-linking circles of the celestial sphere (horizons, meridians, equator) reproduced in three-dimensions by means of metal hoops standing on a stone base. Their function was essentially to study the movement of the stars, and the sun in particular. The various markings also included the hours. Dondi's "astrarium" may have been a combination of ancient and modern knowledge but it represented, above all, a crucial stage in technical development. Time thus ceased to be an abstract and ungraspable idea and became a measurement based on absolute values.

The measurement of time gradually came to be associated with the movements of the stars.

The megaliths of Stonehenge are the most striking and bulky example of a "star clock", calendar and armillary sphere. Priests used Stonehenge to foresee eclipses, impress the common people and sustain their role as mediators between the heavens and the earth, between men and gods, thereby also consolidating their authority.

For the same reasons, the aristocracy from the Renaissance onwards moved these hallmarks from the exclusive domain of public and holy places to place them in full view in their own villas and gardens. The most impressive example still

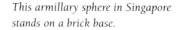

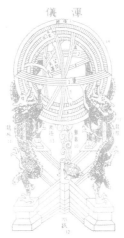

This armillary sphere in Singapore stands on a brick base.

Side: another, much more ancient example (1088) by Su Sung (later remodelled).

Bottom: an arrow acts as the gnomon in this armillary sphere standing in a Swedish garden.

extant is undoubtedly in Jaipur, Rajasthan. The Jantar Mantar is an enormous armillary sphere built by the astronomer Maharajah Jai Sing II around 1730. Standing beside his magnificent palace, this sphere is so large that it is possible to walk between the large stone and marble arches and the complex mechanisms needed to measure the movement of the stars and the moon. The moon's cycle provides a series of references, frequently measured and interpreted by armillary spheres. The moon complete its cyclic phases in about 30 days, the basic calculation for the duration of the months. Moreover, the sexagesimal system, used to calculate minutes and seconds, is precisely 30 multiplied by two. Lastly, the circle –which the Sumerians and Chaldeans associated with the concept of time – is divided into 360 degrees (again a multiple of 30).

A system based on the armillary sphere, although much simpler, has also been used to build portable timepieces. Their dials (also known as the "armillary") indicate the hours of the morning on the left, those of the afternoon on the right, and the time around midday in the centre.

The armillary sphere, with its hoops all but suspended in a void, thus brings together the holy and the profane, science and power, technical skills and art. It also, hanging between sky and earth, inter-relates the immensely small with the immensely huge.

155

Sundials and armillary spheres

The sundial is the only instrument that always indicates true local time, which differs from place to place. The celestial sphere is divided into 24 segments for purely practical reasons, each one marked by the same time (with the few exceptions being mostly for political reasons). As soon as we move over the surface of the Earth from one meridian to another, time changes. Even after only a few metres, time is different from that at the starting point. The term "meridian" derives from the Latin word for "midday", which highlights that this instrument – the sundial – is only able to perform its task during daylight hours. Sundials may indicate not only the hours but also other information, such as the passage between the signs of the Zodiac. The time may be calculated directly (the number indicated matches the hour) or indirectly. For example, such dials may indicate the time left until sunset or the hours passed since dawn.

Over the centuries, a huge range of sundials has been developed. From the Roman Empire through to the XIII century, time was measured from dawn to dusk, dividing the day into 12 hours which were longer or shorter depending on the season. The shortest hours were in winter (about 45 minutes), the longest in summer (about 75 minutes). The first hour matched dawn, the third mid-morning, the sixth midday, the ninth mid-afternoon and the twelfth sunset. Mention is made of these in holy books and in the rules of monasteries. They are also known as unequal, temporal, Biblical or Judaic hours. Later, the sundial with Babylonian (or ab ortu) hours came into use, wherein the 24 hours had a constant duration and were counted from sunrise (as in ancient Babylon); midday coincided with the peak of the sun over the local meridian.

Obviously, the hours marked

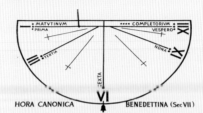

HORA CANONICA BENEDETTINA (Sec VII)

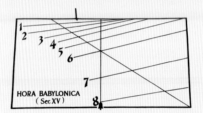

HORA BABYLONICA (Sec XV)

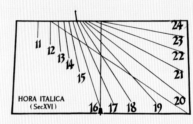

HORA ITALICA (SecXVI)

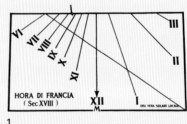

HORA DI FRANCIA (Sec XVIII)

1

1. Various kinds of dials.

2. Polar stylus and normal stylus for sundials on vertical walls.

3. The Sunflower, a sculpture by Giuseppe Ferlenga made up of various sundials.

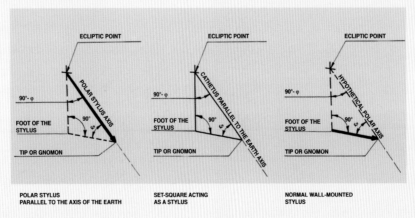

POLAR STYLUS PARALLEL TO THE AXIS OF THE EARTH

SET-SQUARE ACTING AS A STYLUS

NORMAL WALL-MOUNTED STYLUS

2

3

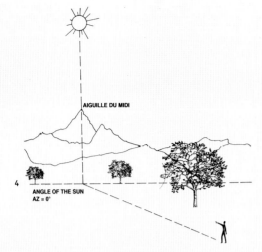

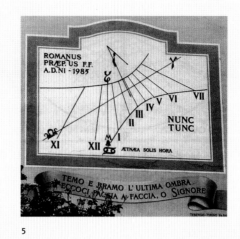

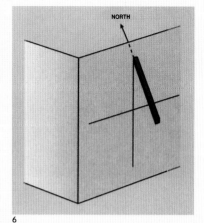

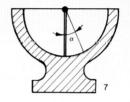

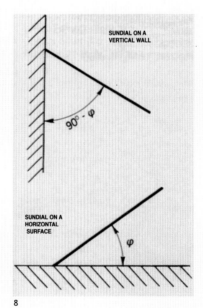

different times of day in summer and winter. As Arab culture spread throughout the Mediterranean area, so time came to be measured from sunset, as was the tradition in the Orient. Sundials with Italic (or ab occasu) hours remained in use until the mid-1800s. Here, the 24 hours had a constant duration; the first began after sunset and marked the beginning of the day. Last century saw the spread, initially in France and later in Piedmont and the rest of Italy, of sundials marking "French hours" (also defined as modern, astronomic or European). This type is by now the most common since it is also the easiest to interpret. The 24 hours have a constant duration and counting begins from midnight. The time indicated is thus closer to that shown by mechanical clocks. All types of sundials have hour lines, straight lines showing the hour; daytime lines are curved (except for the line of the equinox) and indicate the date and the signs of the Zodiac. Other lines had special functions: such as lines of the equator or the equinox, crossed by the shadow of the tip of the

gnomon to indicate spring and autumn equinoxes; the line of the solstice, with a more or less accentuated hyperbolic design depending on the latitude; the figure-of-8 lemniscate line used to distinguish between true summer time and the time indicated by mechanical clocks. Some sundials also have many original features, such as the canonical dial standing in front of the Pailas Royal in Paris, which is fitted with a lens which focuses the rays of the sun on a detonator at midday so that a shot is fired. Armillary spheres are astronomical instruments shaped like a globe, they stylus of which corresponds to the axis of the Earth. There are various scaled and mobile hoops, inside each other, which help determine the position of a celestial body and, indirectly, the passing of time. When the armillary sphere is intended simply to indicate the time, it is simplified into a single hemisphere (the lower one) with a gnomon in the centre.

4. The sun and the land have been placed in close relationship since Antiquity.

5. A wall-mounted sundial in Limone, Cuneo, Italy, with a polar stylus and French hour lines.

6. Setting a polar stylus.

7. Cross-section and axonometry of the scaphius, the instrument used by Heratosthene to measure the length of the meridian.

8. The gnomons of vertical and horizontal "clocks". The angle depends on the local latitude.

9. Example of a gnomon parallel to the base wall.

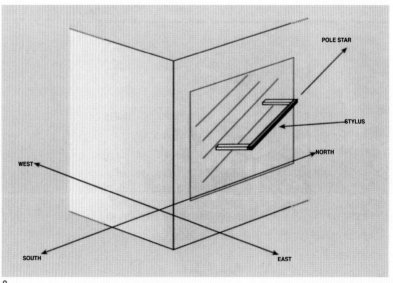

SHUTTERS AND
OTHER CLOSURES
BALUSTERS AND
PARAPETS
WINDOWS
BALCONIES
DORMERS AND
ROOF-TERRACES

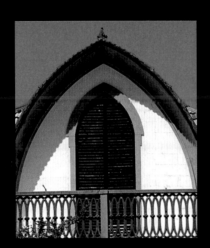
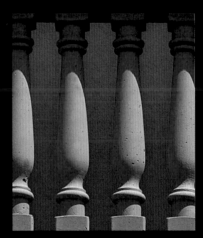

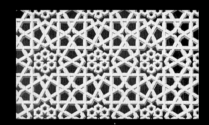

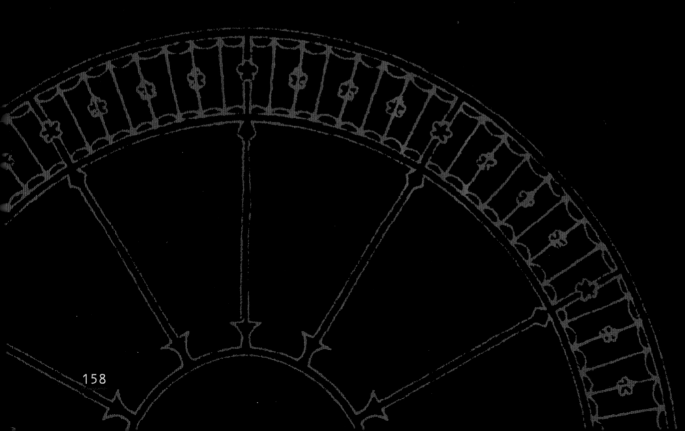

Screens

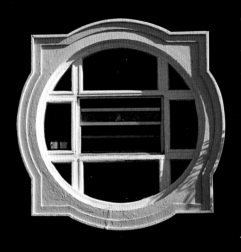

Separating two worlds – the outside, public world of streets and squares and the inside, private and sacred world –screens may be physical or even virtual barriers.

Be they doors, balconies, windows, railings or the like, they exemplify man's desire to meet his equals, discover the surrounding world and, effectively, establish relationships with the outside world. Their thresholds mediate between public and private areas but, at the same time, they protect privacy. Throughout the Orient and in Islamic countries, there are few, or only very narrow, windows overlooking the street. Such openings are hidden by dense gratings or classical shutters that prevent the women of the house being seen by strangers, just as the Islamic veil hides that which only the man of the house is allowed to admire.

In the XV century, Leon Battista Alberti wrote that a door should be "harmonised with the stature of men, and twice as high as wide". This need for magnificence, then and now, inspired the innumerable and imaginative decorations that came to characterise the essential functions of these structures.

Ornamentation became an integral part of the design and construction of screens, - themselves necessary and irreplaceable – thereby providing "added value". In reality, windows and balconies are simply voids, empty spaces that only position, form and decoration can qualify. Vitruvian, Palladian, Serlian… their names recall famous designers. Each treatise classified these screens and the parapets which protected them, be they gratings, railings or various and articulated balusters. They were immensely popular in the Baroque age and almost completely forgotten in the Neo-Classic period.

Climate, sunlight, technology and materials have always influenced the design of screens. For instance, glass, known since Antiquity, only became common in the Renaissance – up until then a variety of other materials were used. One of the most highly-prized was alabaster which, when sliced into thin slabs, allows a warm, amber light to filter through it. Screens thus protect us from the outside while also enabling us to observe it.

Shutters and other closures

See but not be seen: this was the purpose of the stone gratings installed in the courtyards of Isfahan, Iran, held dear by the women who were often obliged to stay indoors.

It was known as early as the XV century B.C. that heating together sand, soda and lime produced a solid, semi-transparent material. Nonetheless, even many centuries later, when windows were to be enclosed other translucent materials were used. For example, thin slabs of marble, alabaster and mica were used or films made from animal skins or oiled paper. It was only in the Renaissance that the quality of glass improved significantly, achieving true transparency and the possibility of producing panes of some size. Glass was used by the Roman only in their spas, where it let through the light and retained heat. In places with a warm climate and strong light, where the ancient civilisations (Mesopotamia, Egypt, Greece and Rome) had developed, homes generally had only small apertures as the desire was to keep out the heat and light. In addition, the load-bearing structure did not allow the inclusion of large voids. Even when pillars and columns were invented, windows remained small. In Roman villas, windows were mostly arranged around the central courtyard (atrium) and it was by no means rare that external walls were entirely "blind".

In northern Europe, on the other hand, where the climate was radically different, large openings were required to ensure sufficient illumination, while these windows had to be suitably screened to retain artificial heat during winter months. A compromise was achieved in the Romanesque period, especially in religious architecture, through a new approach to working stone. Fretwork was developed, which meant that large, intricate panels could be used to enclose a large aperture. Each hole in the fretworked material was closed by a tile of glass secured with lead. The result was a multitude of small panes, at times coloured, held together by tiny structural elements. In the Gothic period, this system came to be used even in public buildings, which thus enjoyed new expressive scope.

In the 1400s, the new Humanist movement brought about a wind of change that even embraced technology. Glass windowpanes held together by strips of lead became common at this time and were used to enclose larger areas. Transparency was still far from perfect but interiors were nevertheless much better illuminated than before. Sliding windows appeared in France in the mid-1600s; at the same time, panes of glass measuring four square metres were being produced and the metal support frames consequently became smaller. This helped

An orange band highlights this simple window in Oman.

A window becomes a major compositional element throughout the facade, with embrasures, orders and tympanums: Islamic influences are evident even in Jerusalem.

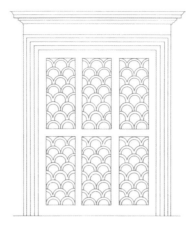

Below: these gratings in Ghardaia, in the Algerian desert, are intended to provide ventilation while screening out sunlight.

Red is the dominant colour of the fittings in the Forbidden City, Peking, these– unlike those in the desert – can be opened.

Centre: gratings made up of half-moon elements in wood or stone.

Side: a Persian shutter in Villa Visconti Brignano, near Bergamo, Italy. The blue wood contrasts with the red of the crowning shell decoration.

improve the effects of delicacy and airiness, as well as the amount of light penetrating the room – and the chance to look curiously inside. The need to balance sunlight and privacy was always important and gave rise to various design solutions. Examples of external wooden shutters with fixed vertical and horizontal slats were a common feature of Roman homes, where they were used as a screen against the strong sunlight. In the Near East and North Africa, gratings were more common, made using criss-cross structures comprising bars of metal or, more frequently, strips of wood. During the Moghul period in India, stone gratings, with delicate lace-like decorations, were employed to cover the entire aperture. Yet the queen of such screens and enclosures is the Persian shutter, an external fitting common in Middle East countries which became popular in Europe in the 1700s. These shutters are made of parallel slats of wood, installed at an angle to allow the flow of air but keep out sunlight (and unwanted gazers). They may be mobile with two parts opening outward, have several fold-up sections like a book, slide in and out of chambers in the main wall or roll-up inside a caisson inside the room itself. The end part of the Persian shutter was often known as a modesty panel because it allowed women to look out over the street without being seen. Solid or blind shutters were used in Europe for much the same purpose and were occasionally fold-up designs. Venetian blinds were shutters that could be rolled up from the inside; they were equally effective in protecting privacy and allowing those inside to see without being seen.

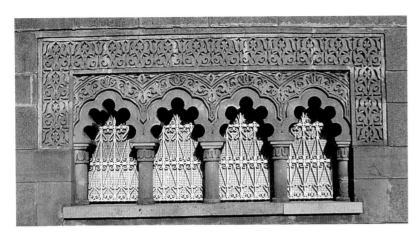

Modern gratings and ancient architecture blend harmoniously in this building in Rabat, Morocco.

Lanterns, colours and creativity characterise this colonial architecture in the centre of Singapore. It blends perfectly with the Chinese style which predominates even outside "Chinatown".

Balusters and parapets

This wooden balcony is in Zanzibar, where European and Arab styles blend admirably.

Balusters are architectural structures formed by a sequence of small pillars inserted between the base and the handrail. The term "baluster" derives from the Greek *balaústion*, "pomegranate flower", the shape of which was taken as a model for these small stone or wooden pillars, which generally had one or two tapering, round or polygonal segments with undulations or other shapes. The proportions and details of the elements may vary significantly and there is no relationship between different orders and different kinds of baluster. A sequence of balusters creates a parapet having decorative and functional purposes. The composition is flanked by pillars resembling the pedestals of orders used in facades. The height of the balusters is determined by these basic elements; it is usual to match balusters with the order of the floor where they are installed. The more decorated or subtle the order, the more the baluster tends to emphasise lightness. Many different compositional rules were followed and classified at various times in history. Sixteenth century essayist Filippo Baldinucci, in his *Tuscan Glossary of the Arts of Design*, mentions that "it is customary to reinforce the orders of balusters with a number of pillars placed at convenient intervals". Neo-Classic critics were damning in their judgement of this component, so much so that Antoine Chrysostome Quatrèmere de Quincy, one of the most authoritative critics of the early 1800s, in his dictionary of architecture, defined them as a "wretched invention". Such distaste arose from the indiscriminate use of balusters. The baluster, because it has a practical function, also developed in far-flung cultures, though it was, admittedly, modified in relation to local styles. In South East Asia, for example, the place of the baluster is often taken by the naga, a religious motif derived from Buddhist art (it means "snake").

The parapet, on the other hand, is a more general term, used to describe a structure of 70-110 centimetres in height made of a variety of materials, which was installed as protection on balconies, terraces and stairs. Parapets may be solid, fret-worked or made of railings. Solid parapets are in simple masonry, stone or marble and may be decorated with tiles or bas-reliefs. Fret-worked parapets may have a huge variety of designs – floral, geometrical, animalesque – depending on the period and the area.

Railings are used as parapets in staircases and in some cases even to crown buildings in place

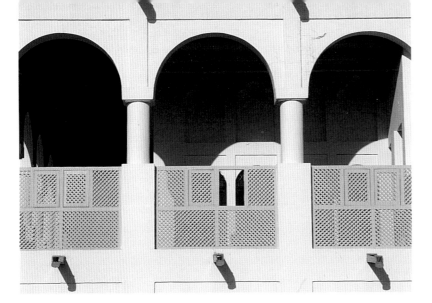

Gratings as delicate as lace once provided a screen against indiscreet observation in this villa at Doha, Qatar, today the National Museum.

A pure white balustrade outlines a terrace in Puerto Cabello, Venezuela.

An elegant flowered Liberty design by architect Giuseppe Sommaruga for the Casa Castiglioni in Milan.

Wood and colour: maximum simplicity for maximum effect in Cusco, not far from Machu Picchu, Peru.

Slim, elongated balusters on a balcony in Puerto Cabello, Venezuela.

More balusters, this time more classical in style, in a 1900s villa at Palm Beach, Florida.

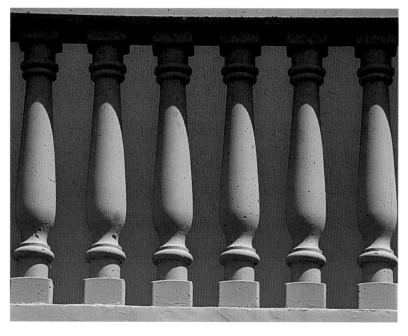

A sequence of balusters adorning balconies in Cusco. The Peruvian Andes are clearly visible in the background thanks to the clear, high-altitude air.

"Imported" Liberty styling for this impressive open balcony in the centre of Lima, Peru.

of an attic. They may be in marble or stone, bronze or wood. While balusters became common in Italian architecture in the 1400s-1500s, in northern Europe the preference was still for parapets made up of gratings and railings. Such railings enjoyed their peak of glory in the Romanesque period. They remained popular until the Renaissance and were subsequently replaced by balusters. However, the tradition continued in England until the XVI century; here parapets were used to define balconies and staircases. It was customary to add rich Baroque decorations with naturalistic motifs, especially in wood, made by expert wood carvers whose skill has rarely been bettered. From the 1500s, the term railings came to indicate a structure in a variety of materials and designs providing spatial protection. Railings came to be distinguished from parapets by being lighter and much less solid. The use of iron, in particular, achieves impressive effects thanks to its workability.

There is also another form of parapet known as the Polish style, so-named because it was used to crown numerous 1500s buildings in Poland. These involve blind arches with pinnacles and other motifs crowning a facade in order to hide the rood. They are very similar to attics.

Slim columns and a dense network of wooden strips characterise this balcony in Muscat, Oman.

Rajasthan is still home to craftsmen capable of working stone like lace; this is one of the many examples that can be admired in Jaisalmer.

VILLA DETAILS

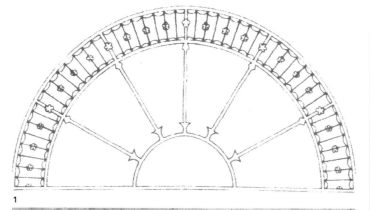

1

2

3

5

4

21

22   23

24   25

9

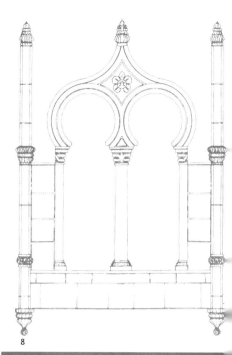

8

6   26   27   28   29   7   30

Windows

We must be able to enter a building before we can look outside, consequently doors were originally more important than windows. In the "first house" of our infancy, the door is the principal threshold between the intimate and enclosed space at the centre of our known and reassuring world and the unknown, sometimes threatening entities that surround us. Yet windows soon gain great importance, both from the inside, as a source of ventilation, light and vision, and from the outside, as a decorative and compositional element. Windows, through their shape, proportions, size, sequence and the interplay of solid and open spaces often emerge as the main architectural element in a facade. From the rose windows of Christian cathedrals through to contemporary buildings, windows are a crescendo of voids in solid masonry. In this way, solid and empty spaces combine equally to define the overall composition.

Windows may be arched or framed, plain or richly decorated, kiosk-like or Rococo, traditionally high and narrow or in the broad, landscape style of more recent times. Opening on to the world as a means of observation, communication and even exhibition, windows interpret different building styles, tastes and trends. Windows are made up of the opening itself; the sill or lower edge, which may be enlarged to resemble a threshold and at times even overhangs the main face of the building; the jambs or uprights (side members) and the architrave or lintel (top beam), respectively for straight and arched windows.

Windows, in the ultimate analysis, are merely holes in a larger structure, a void, something "missing" marked off by the window itself. On the one hand, this involves the technical capacity of the wall to incorporate gaps and, conversely, a morphological definition of the wall itself. These two aspects are joined by a third component: the mobile window fitting, which closes the opening and restores a certain degree of continuity to the main structure. This component has its own capabilities and uses and thus contributes towards defining the functional, technological and semantic performance of the window as such.

The history of windows is long and fascinating. Their evolution is linked with the materials and static-construction systems used in different places and periods. The most ancient window is the one mentioned in the Book of Genesis. God suggested to Noah that he create

Above: in stone or stuccowork, window frames became much more elaborate in the Baroque age.

Following page: an intricate trompe-l'oeil framing a simple window in Zeil, Germany.

17

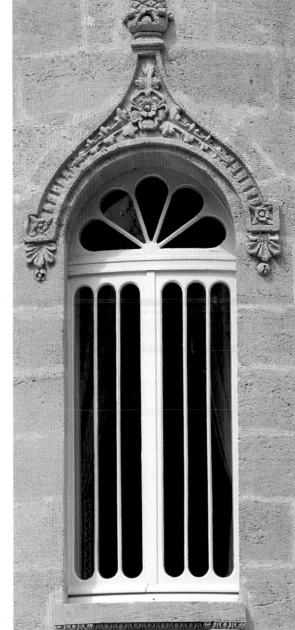

20

37 38 18 39 40 19 41 4

10

16

15

32

12

33

34

13

35

14

36

an aperture in the Ark so that the Dove of Peace could be released. The Bible also mentions that the Tabernacle in the Temple of Solomon was surrounded by windows which were wide on the inside and narrow on the exterior. Windows developed from the primitive openings made in the tents of nomads (barely screened by strips of woven animal skin), through slits, then architraved windows and the first double and triple mullioned windows, to windows with supporting sills and ledges made up of delicate scrolls in axis with the jambs. The advent of reinforced concrete and steel helped make once unthinkable artistry now commonplace and introduced new concepts, even in residential building.

The banded landscape window, symbolising the modern movement, was taken up by Le Corbusier in the Ronchamp Chapel, only he broke it down again into dozens of small apertures which create an unusual symphony of light and shade. It is no coincidence that the famous architect was wont to claim that all his architecture was designed around windows.

Windows soon took on different names and styles, such as the well-known Palladian window with its broad semi-circles arranged over three sectors; Serlian windows, perhaps closer to loggias than windows; and the eclectic compositions of the 1800s-1900s. Nor should we forget the rhythmic scanning of windows in the Gothic period: while changing from floor to floor and fully responding to the needs imposed by the interior, they equally graced facades in an harmonious and striking manner. The vertical axes and strict symmetry of Renaissance windows embraced architectural orders, strips, columns, tympanums and trabeations – all of which configured strong links between the facade's proportions and rhythm and the laws of harmony which govern the entire Universe. Such concepts echo the atmospheres, necessities and sumptuousness of the past.

Windows are thus both an instrument and a concept: their continuous morphological mutations have merely followed the trends of the times. Windows have always aroused interest, admiration and, at times, even mischievous curiosity.

Balconies

The history of balconies is closely linked with the history of windows. If windows embody the relationship with the outside world, then balconies highlight this function to the utmost. If architecture was initially content with a simple aperture, this opening was later expanded and elaborated to the point of transforming a functional element into a decorative motif.

Balconies may be considered as windows that extend at floor level through an element, however small, which overhangs the facade, often supported by brackets, and protected by railings, parapets or balusters. Such balconies may be very small or very large, to the point of embracing the entire facade.

Balconies are known as galleries when they are not only large but also perform a particularly

A typical Indian balcony topped by an arch. This building is the Badal Mahal, one of the finest mansions in Jaisalmer, Rajasthan.

Slender corbels support this solid balcony in the Colossi fortress, Cyprus.

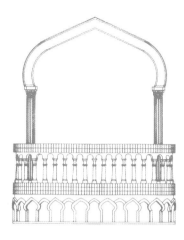

An ogival arch frames a balcony in a mansion in Oman, Persian Gulf.

These two balconies, designed by Gaudi in Casa Battló, Barcelona, look almost like human faces.

important functional and representational role. Layouts are immensely varied: at times, balconies stand over the main door, at others they are widened to embrace two or more windows, sometimes they extend along the entire facade of the building and may even continue around the corners.

While balconies are a more recent decorative element than windows, their origins are nevertheless rather ancient and many examples are to be found in certain Roman villas in Ostia (the old port of Rome).

Between the 1400s and 1500s, balconies were commonly installed in a basement area jutting out from the main facade or above the storey-marker cornice, as well as on top of columns with a trabeation. In the same period, support embrasures and balusters underwent significant and highly creative design developments that helped embellish the structure of the balcony, creating a fundamental motif in the "personality" of the facade. This trend was all the more emphasised in the Baroque period, when balconies were transformed into true jewels of ornamental sculpture.

Highly-decorative, sinuous balusters were later joined by iron railings, which made it possible to pursue stylistic research culminating in the delicate and superbly elegant lace-work wrought iron railings created by master craftsmen. Columns were often replaced by caryatids and hermae, while flowers, leaves, volutes, scrolls, shields and masques competed with each other to create the unique, almost living elements which richly enlivened facades. Balconies may or may not have ledges (the latter are smaller and less

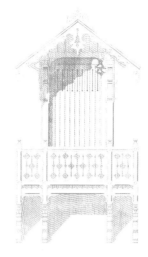

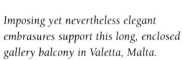

Imposing yet nevertheless elegant embrasures support this long, enclosed gallery balcony in Valetta, Malta.

A roof balcony in the former British colony of Belize. Vaguely in the Victorian style, it is made entirely of wood.

Liberty and Baroque styles blend admirably in this balcony in Lima, Peru.

Echoes of the colonial Spanish Baroque style survive in this modern architecture in Miami, where colour is the main identifying element.

A broad balcony in the centre of
Catania, Sicily.

The architecture in Santa Fe, New
Mexico, is based on form and –
especially – colour. Strong, contrasting
shades create a delightful atmosphere
in the historic centre of this graceful
city.

Different styles and periods blend in
the mansions of the nouveaux riches in
Palm Beach, Florida.

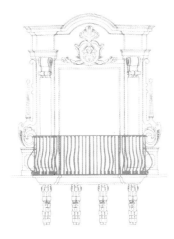

A balcony on the island of Zanzibar, for centuries an African colony of the Sultanate of Oman.

A typical Italian balcony. Balconies became more elaborate and striking in the Baroque period.

Below, left: a small balcony on the inside facade of the Vanderbilt mansion, Long Island, New York.

Below, right: balconies are common in the Seychelles, although they are always covered against the frequent tropical downpours.

frequent). At times, the overhang is small or otherwise minimises the projection from the main wall.

Suspended balconies, on the other hand, may project out of the line of the facade and be supported by embrasures or columns and vaults.

The load-bearing structure in early balconies was in wood and involved two beams set into the masonry on which the base platform, also made from wooden planks, was placed. The term originates from the German word *Balken*, meaning

Balconies in modern Chinese architecture are especially decorative, such as this example in Taipei, Taiwan.

A combination of Spanish and Mexican styles, this balcony dominates Ocean Drive in Miami Beach.

"beam". In the Middle Ages, support embrasures came into to use with cornices having one or more courses, especially for slightly overhanging balconies.

In the past, overhanging balconies were rarely large because of the limitations imposed by the materials used. With the introduction of reinforced concrete, these limitations were largely eliminated and new expressive opportunities were encouraged.

Balconies with slabs supported by embrasures are the most common type and provide the greatest number of historical examples, especially those with marble or stone slabs and support brackets. There are also balconies standing on columns or vaults, which, depending on the degree of elaboration, often create a kind of pronaos which emphasises the main door.

Closed balconies or bow-windows combine the features of both elements and are typical of Tudor architecture in England in the 1400s and 1500s. They share many features with Islamic and Middle Eastern architecture and it is no coincidence that this style is common throughout the eastern Mediterranean area.

Neither doors nor windows, balconies merge the formal characteristics of both components to become a hybrid, which came and went down the centuries depending on "cultural" climates and latitudes. They are a constant, yet variable, element in villas throughout the world.

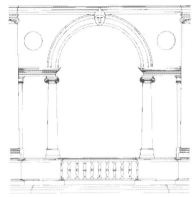

Prominent, elegant and almost exclusively decorative: this balcony in Reykjavik can be used for only a few days in the year.

A typical Palladian design in Vicenza: three apertures separated by two columns supporting an arch.

Villa Vimercati Scotti in Gallarate, Italy. The facade has three balconies surmounted by curved tympanums.

Dormers and roof-terraces

The architecture of Northern Europe is characterised by dormers, found in many residential buildings, be they villas, palaces or town houses.

Sharply sloping roofs, necessary to ensure rainwater run-off and avoid accumulation of snow, create large loft-like areas often of liveable dimensions. It was to avoid wasting such space that the first attic-lofts were developed as a means of exploiting these habitable areas.

In his *Tuscan Glossary of the Arts of Design*, Filippo Baldinucci mentions that dormers are used "to illuminate rooms otherwise confined to darkness and also to gain access to the roof". Dormers have always provided greater protection against the infiltration of rainwater than skylights or roof windows.

Large enough to hold a room, this dormer defines the roof of a mansion in La Digue, Seychelles

They were considered as a more elegant decorative motif which also helped formally define the facade, especially because they lightened the compact mass of the roof inevitable in such buildings.

In some instances, dormers were characterised by strips, tympanums, arches and other decorative elements which enhanced elegance at the same time as emphasising sturdiness and stability in a manner that a simple roof window is unable to achieve. Roof windows, in fact, were used only to provide natural lighting in transit areas, small lofts and store-rooms. At times, the slope of the roof was such that several dormers were installed on top of the other. The installation of a dormer involves a full-scale interruption of the roof, inserting an element quite separate from the roof. The dormer was, itself, covered by two roofing slopes and has a window providing light and views. Dormers allow a wide range of dimensional and formal designs, so much so that at times they are finished off by a small balcony set into the roof itself. Balconies of this kind have always been popular, not the least because of the "control", if not actual defence possibilities, they offer. Dormers have thus been successfully joined by other projecting windows – such as bow, bay and Oriel windows. Perhaps inspired by Mediaeval turrets, these may even be large and become rather like lounges. When they have large glass areas, their defensive purpose is obviously sacrificed in favour of better interior illumination. As for roof terraces, these atypical windows create a link between the inside and outside worlds, providing functions impossible for simple windows and becoming

Small yet elegant, this contemporary dormer is in Miami Beach.

Delicate volutes flank this simple dormer on the Caribbean island of Trinidad. The plain two-colour design contrasts with the darker roofing slate.

Mediterranean classicism and northern influences combine in this dormer in Prague.

Skilfully carved stone creates slender and striking designs in this Danish castle.

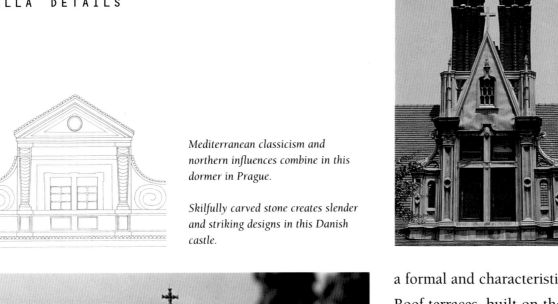

A dormer and chimney-stacks merge on the roof of Cohen Hall, Long Island, New York.

Mid-way between a dormer and a roof terrace, this exploitable roof embellishes a mansion in Maderia.

a formal and characteristic hallmark of villas.

Roof terraces, built on the roofs of buildings, are essentially exploitable areas with a slight slope to ensure rainwater run-off, they are protected by a parapet and accessible from inside the building.

When there are no inner courtyards, roof terraces provide access to an outside area without leaving the privacy of the home, although they are not entirely protected from indiscreet observation. Certain frescoes of the 1400s suggest that roof terraces were especially used by women to hang out the washing. It was only later, in the Mannerist and, particularly, the Baroque periods, that they became a characteristic formal element of the entire building. Roof terraces emphasise the vertical impact of the composition

The colour of the stone contrasts strongly with the green patina of this copper roof in Frediriksborg, Hillerod, Denmark.

Natural light was provided in large lofts in the palaces of Prague by installing numerous and imposing dormers.

Simple and original dormers in Shirley Heights, Antigua.

and disguise part of the roof, while the balusters become a decorative element where coats of arms and inscriptions can be installed.

Roof terraces are not common in northern countries, for obvious climatic reasons. In contrast, in warm and dry climates – such as pre-Sahara desert areas and the Persian Gulf – the entire roof is transformed into a terrace, blending with the roofing system. This new hybrid is still a characteristic feature in the landscape of many towns and villages. In warm and wet tropical climates, on the other hand, this detail has always followed the trends imposed by colonists, usually merging with belvedere turrets and galleries.

Dormers, roof-terraces and balconies

A dormer is a habitable area created beneath the roof, though it may project somewhat above the level of the roof itself; it is designed to provide lighting for the rooms underneath the roof and also to gain access to the outside part of the roofing system. Dormers may be semi-circular, round (with round windows), or have two sloping roofs covering the abutting portion.
Dormers stand above the main cornice or roof impost. The rooms have a trapezoidal cross-section with sloped ceilings following the angle of the roof.
The most common dormers are exploitable areas and may even become full-scale lofts or mansards, named after French architects François Mansart and Jules Hardouin-Mansart, who made widespread use of this feature in the XVII century.
Dormers originated with the ancient French "baie" (window chambers); these elements were common in the Gothic Age and remained in use until the Renaissance, especially in northern Europe.
Roof terraces are habitable areas raised above the roof, but they do not project over the facade (otherwise they would become balconies). In some cases, a roof terrace is a simple viewpoint or covered passageway used as a belvedere or solarium, also providing access to the roof. Early examples appeared in the 1400s in Italy, although large-scale development only took place in the Baroque palaces of Papal Rome.
When roof terraces project out from the main body of the building they are really balconies, which may be large, small or even enclosed galleries. The overhang is achieved by a platform, which may or may not be supported by embrasures. Embrasures are rather important in the composition of balconies, since the marble slabs, stone or brick base – until the advent of reinforced

1. A partitioned balcony in the Ducal Palace, Urbino.

2. The steep roof of this mansion in the Seychelles has become a large loft illuminated by two dormers.

3. An engraving of the late 1700s by Giuseppe Zocchi depicts the Poggio Imperiale Villa in Florence.

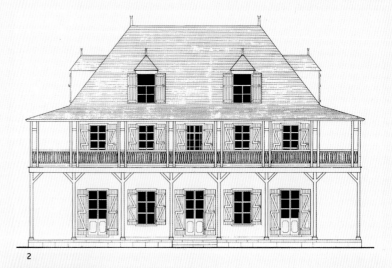

4

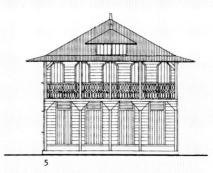

5

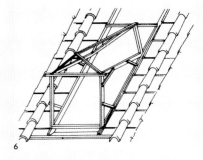

6

concrete – always required the support of metal or stone "brackets". Other design solutions include balconies supported by trabeations, in turn standing on columns, generally over the main door. At times, the columns are replaced by caryatids. Closed balconies or galleries are a separate category and perhaps derive from Roman loggias. Unusual in Italy, they were immensely important in northern European countries, such as England – where they developed into bow-windows. The latter made their return to Europe and some colonies, where they blended with similar Islamic traditions. Dormers, roof terraces and balconies all share parapets, which may be solid or fret-worked and with small balusters, or else involve railings in cast iron, other metal or wood.

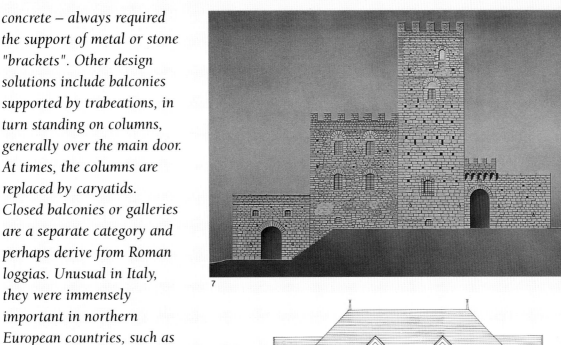

7

4, 5. Two examples of roofs with "mansards" and dormers.

6. The classic structure of dormers.

7. The tower of Villa Pratelli in Tuscany was converted into a roof terrace last century.

8, 9, 10. Examples of loft roofs inspired by French architecture in the Seychelles. Large dormers provide natural lighting for the interiors.

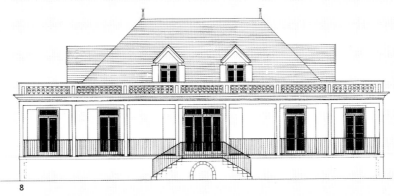

8

9

10

DOORS

DOORFRAMES

CLAPPERS AND

DOORBELLS

GATES

PORTALS

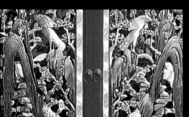

Mankind has always felt the "animal" urge to "mark" his territory and delineate his private spaces. Doors are one of the most important elements in any building; they define the division between two worlds: the external, public world and the internal, intimate and protected private world. Thresholds have thus always played a symbolic, if not religious role. Recalling Scilla and Cariddis or the columns of Hercules on a private scale, doors – more pragmatically speaking – maintain the privacy of villas by excluding outsiders and impostors, the merely curious and the time-wasters.

Since Antiquity, the need has been felt to characterise entrances in formal terms, so much so that they may even indicate the social status of the owners and keep pace with architectural trends. The entrance to a villa must interpret the taste and culture of the owners, indicate wealth and also act as a "filter" and protective element. Small, medium and large doors, gates and portals have always characterised the facades of important buildings. Their design includes orders, tympanums, gables and even busts, coats of arms, epigraphs, shields and festoons in an orgy of symbols and embellishment, which, at times, have no purpose other than decoration. In the Baroque period, in particular, doors became the very emblem of the architecture of the building and every mansion had to be preceded by an imposing entrance.

In the same way, doors also interpret the taste and wealth of the owner, by using costly woods and materials and involving fine metal decorations.

Clappers, doorbells, bosses and hinges decorate doors like the precious jewellery worn by the lady of the house. Clappers or doorknockers once announced visitors and, although today replaced by video-entry phones, they bear witness to long-lost customs and the ancient protective role of doors and doorways.

Doors

Doors are openings through the thickness of a wall that provide access to the interior of a building. The appearance of doors depends on the structural and formal solutions employed in their construction. A distinction is made between doorways and gates in terms of size and the elegance of decoration. The major role played by doors in the formal characterisation of facades is emphasised by the careful alternation of solids and voids which, together with windows, define the spatial arrangement of the entire building system.

Doors can be divided into three categories depending on their structural system. The most common type is the trilyptic door, where the architrave discharges forces on to side pillars or jambs, thereby eliminating any lateral stress. Arched doors, on the other hand, make it possible to embrace larger spans without intermediate supports, although the blocks of stone in the arch itself are subject to compression forces which are discharged – both vertically and laterally – on to the side jambs. Lastly, certain arched doorways are set into a rectangular opening where the arched vault overlaps the architrave of the enclosed chamber.

One of the doors to the Royal Palace in Ayuttaya, the ancient capital of the Kingdom of Thailand.

In the Mediterranean area, the most common style is based on the trilyptic doorway and the space thereby defined may be rectangular or vaguely trapezoidal. In ancient Egypt, as can still be seen in certain tombs and temples, the architrave was supported not by pillars but by the blocks of stone incorporated into the main wall, although the static principle is much the same. The pillar-architrave system stands out from the line of the wall and is decorated, mostly with hieroglyphics but also by coloured inserts. Other decorations involving grooved patterns recall earlier wooden systems.

Tryliptic trapezoidal stone doors are generally more ancient and various examples are to be found, especially on the island of Malta. In Minoan Greece, jambs were generally in wood decorated with painted bands, while in the Mycenean period, rectangular or trapezoidal doorways were in marble and stone and were at times outlined by semi-columns. Although similar static systems were employed in Persia, the general trend was to decorate the inside of the jambs with bas-reliefs. The Etruscans preferred trapezoidal openings but equally perfected the arched doorway, already in use in Mesopotamia from the VIII century B.C. Decorations were limited to friezes around the architrave and jambs, with occasional bas-reliefs. It was only much later that doors came to include elements of the classic architectural

This door in Iceland resembles a temple. The door and frame are all in wood.

This colourful and unusual contemporary door in Sana'a, Yemen, on the other hand, is entirely in metal.

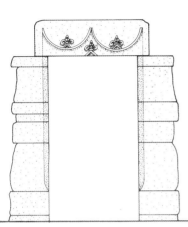

A XIII century stone doorway in France.

Lacquered and gilt wood of evident Chinese inspiration in the cosmopolitan city of Penang, northern Malaysia.

This framed door surviving in Gardaia, Algeria, bears witness to a much more glorious past.

orders imported from Greece.

Since the load-bearing walls were in stone and were very thick, the architrave of the doorway had to withstand very high loads. To avoid the need for massive beams, the load discharge triangle was introduced; this was a kind of tympanum above the doorway itself which helped support the weight of the wall above and discharged thrust forces laterally. This system never entirely disappeared and came back into fashion in various periods, at times even in the form of a load-bearing arch above the architrave itself.

The Romans, in particular, exploited the capacities of the arch-vaulted doorway, especially in residential buildings. Town gates and, above all, triumphal arches often incorporated the niche above the doorway, with the arch set into an architectural order culminating with a horizontal cornice and a triangular fronton. From the IV century, doors and windows came to be much more highly decorated; the Hellenic tradition was reviewed and at time re-invented, so that the profiles of mouldings increasingly abandoned the canons of strict classicism to discover new equilibriums and new proportions. The Imperial Age was a time of great artistic vitality, when Roman villas became richer and more perfect, achieving unequalled splendour. The entrances to these mansions clearly depict the splendours hidden inside. The Humanist renaissance of the villa could have by no means ignored and emphasised these values which, admittedly to different extents, ultimately became the *leitmotiv* of mansions in the rest of Europe and in the colonies.

Richly decorated door panels and an intricate cornice: the mansion may be rather simple but the main doors to homes in Bali are always courtly.

An unusual trapezoidal tympanum in Kashan, Iran.

Form and colour in otherwise dull Iceland. Twin doors highlight different personalities.

Doors

"Doorways" are effectively apertures in the walls of a building which provide access to the interior, while "doors" are also the fittings, generally in wood, which close this passageway. The Latin words for such "entrances" were "porta" and "portus".

The opening itself may be constructed in a variety of ways. The trilyptic doorway is very common in the Mediterranean area and was described by Vitruvius in his treatise De architectura; it involves two jambs supporting an architrave which, in turn, supports the overlying wall. Arched doorways, initially used by the Assyrians and Babylonians, were later developed and classified by the Romans. The true arch, unlike the pseudo-arch, owes its significant stability to the counter-action of thrust forces exerted on the stone building blocks which cancel each other out. There are several variants, such as the pointed arch common in the Gothic Age and the horseshoe arch typical of Muslim architecture.

The pseudo-arch is a combination of these two; it, like the pseudo-vault, is supported by overlapping blocks of stone arranged in projection up to the peak of the pyramid thus formed. The load-bearing capacity of this kind of arch is lower than for true arches but nevertheless very considerable. Various megalithic structures and certain Maya temples in Central America have many doorways with pseudo-arches still in exceptional functional condition.

The first architecturally identifiable "doors" were the gates in town walls. In Roman times, these gates were given precise names depending on their location (decumana, gattaia, levatoia, praetoria, principalis, etc.). It was especially in the Renaissance that doorways for private houses assumed a more representative function, to the extent that they were designed with the same attention to detail as the facade. Certain compositional elements, such as tympanums (triangular, curved, mixed and interrupted), columns, strips, shields and so forth were all utilised to achieve formal definition. All the most important essayists

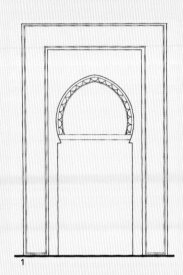

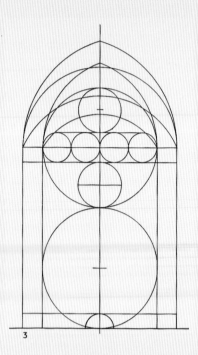

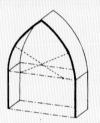

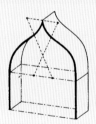

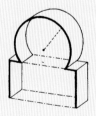

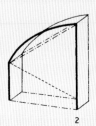

1. A Moorish doorway set into a large, rectangular frame.

2. Various profiles used for doors and gates. From the top: pointed, flamed, redundant and lamed arches.

3. The geometrical composition of an arch-vaulted doorway with a pointed arch.

4. An elegant Liberty-style door.

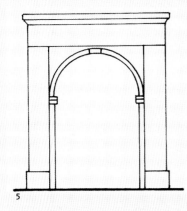

5

contributed to giving doors and doorways a more noble status and certain architects, by chance or by design, later started several "fashions". The "rustic" doors used, for example, in Tuscan architecture by Antonio da Sangallo and later still by Giulio Romano in buildings in Mantua, became the lietmotiv of the Mannerists, so much so that Vignola discussed them extensively in his treatise Regola delli cinque ordini d'architettura (Rules of the Five Orders of Architecture) *published in Rome in 1562.*

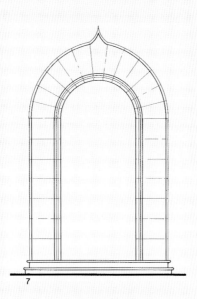

7

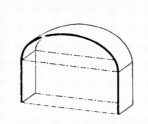

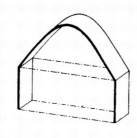

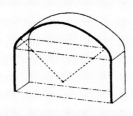

8

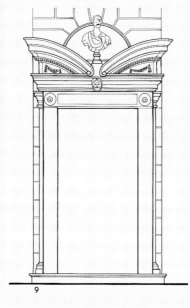

9

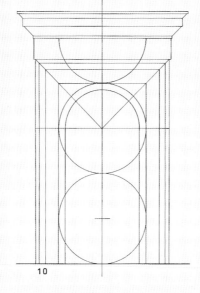

10

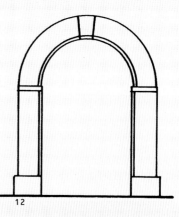

12

5. An arch-vaulted gate set into a rectangular opening.

6. An interrupted, triangular tympanum crowns this door-window.

7. Heavy blocks of stone define this Florentine Renaissance door.

8. Other profiles of doors and gates. From the top: elliptical, parabolic, multi-centred, Tudor.

9. A late 1500s gate by Bernardo Buontalenti.

10. The composition of an architraved gate.

11. A simple architraved gate.

12. A simple arch-vaulted gate.

13. Different geometrical relationships in the composition of an architraved gate.

6

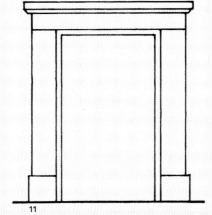

11

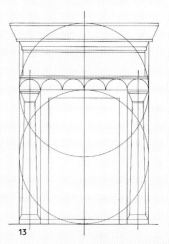

13

Doorframes

Moulding and inlay embellish the fine doors in Qatar, often made from highly prized and perfumed wood.

Elegant doors maintain the privacy of many mansions and villas. Wood, wrought iron or, occasionally, stone create rigid geometries, lace-work and other patterns which celebrate nobility and wealth. Today, doors are again very popular status symbols, as well as being highly-regarded, unique and precious examples of the work of master craftsmen. Statues, pinnacles, vases and scrolls are all used to decorate the fittings used to support door panels. In addition, great creative attention is also paid to the doors themselves. Doors open, close, remain ajar, are shut, thrown wide open and slammed. When closed, doors become mysterious, even forbidding, discouraging and haughty, as well as intimate and protective. We go out and come in through doors, or stand undecided on the threshold. We can eavesdrop behind doors, hide smiles or tears; a slammed door means anger, derision … or just a windy day. Doors don't creak so much these days, not even in austere Scottish castles. Whatever the feelings and emotions hidden behind doors, they are nonetheless the entrance to private worlds and inasmuch – like so many other details – also bear witness to culture, power and wealth. A single, double or sliding door, with its handles, locks, hinges and grilles, its panels and decorations, becomes a complex entity capable of characterising every entrance.

The main material used to make doors is wood: prestigious, reliable, strong, functional, safe and elegant. Wood is a living material with texture that changes with the climate, the type of land and the rainfall of the forests where it grew. This is why so many different kinds of wood are used. Some are commonplace, others are rare and highly-prized like teak, now only to be found in Malaysia and Burma, it is extremely strong but also very costly; or sandalwood, widely used in Oman, where its scent – now mixed with incense - is still powerful in the forts of the Sultans. Such woods are almost impossible to procure and are used today almost exclusively for artistic furniture, although once, in the times of Empires, wealthier families could show off their fortunes by using these materials even for doors. Doors and door panels, therefore, communicate messages of wealth and power, as well as providing solid barriers against unwanted intrusion. Heavy bosses in iron or bronze also help protect doors against violation when heavy metal locks do not already perform this function. When the visual effect has to be somewhat lighter, bas-reliefs can be inserted into panels fitted to the door or,

A carved rosette mounted in the middle of a Florentine door.

Metal decorative elements grace this door of a fine mansion in Dubai, Arab Emirates.

Hinges have been modified from merely functional elements into decorative motifs over the centuries and are often made in wrought iron.

A door opening on to one of the many courtyards inside Peruvian palaces dating back to the Spanish period.

Brass: shiny and completely modelled by hand, in this ancient Danish castle.

A large boss. In the Middle Ages, bosses were used to make doors sturdier and prevent them being shouldered open; they later became purely decorative elements.

A delicate metal handle for a door in Poun, South Korea.

A heavy door panel in solid wood strengthened by two rows of bosses opens on to a courtyard in Kashan, Iran.

more rarely, carved directly into the wood of the door itself. Subject matter varies enormously: festoons are very common, with round or oval motifs with stylised petals and leaves. High-reliefs are also sometimes found, where animal and human figures stand out from the background, almost leaping out to greet visitors. When a house was built in Zanzibar, the first item installed was always the door: the more important and wealthy the owner, the more complex the carvings of the door panels. These included quotations from the Koran, considered to be lucky charms, and numerous symbols. The waves of the sea, for example, recalled the travels of Omanite merchants in the doors to their homes; date palms and incense were symbols of plenty and good health; lotus flowers symbolised fertility. Heavy, sharp-pointed bosses then gave these doors a more impressive and fortified appearance. In India, in the areas colonised by the Omanites, these bosses were fitted to prevent elephants breaking down doors with their bulk. There are no elephants in Zanzibar today but travellers of past centuries have left commentaries suggesting that they were once rather common animals on the island. More or less imposing, more or less courtly, finished with bees wax, pigments, oils or paints, smooth or decorated: whatever the appearance of a door, when it opens it welcome visitors into the private and protected world of the home. The key to the door provides access to a reserved microcosm, often a place of great delights. It is always worth glancing at doors before crossing the threshold: they usually provide some idea of what we are likely to see inside.

Door panels in wood but also metal and glass – combining protection and visibility.

Iron, brass and wood combine in this door panel in Nikko, Japan.

Left: a trapezoidal handle reproducing the same decoration as the panel opens this door in a palace in Bangkok.

Above: Even locks can become a design motif, especially when made in wrought iron.

Left: red and gold decorate this Oriental style door in Montreal.

Top: the "key of love". The reference to the chastity belt is evident although, when opened, this lock simply reveals a fine mansion.

Above: function transformed into decoration. These door hinges in Malé, Maldives, delightfully embellish the main structure of the door.

Clappers and doorbells

Wrought iron against a red door in this 1800s doorknocker in Shanghai

It is increasingly rare to hear the characteristic clatter of doorknockers, those metal rings secured by a plate to the main doors of many villas and palaces. "Going over to the window, he shouted: who's knocking down there?" – Boccaccio, as early as the 1300s, bears witness that "ringing doorbells" was already a commonplace action.

In iron, bronze, cast iron and brass, the clapping of knockers on the wood of doors was amplified in the atrium, which acted like a sounding box to announce the arrival of visitors. In the same way, the entire street became involved in events, if only for the simple reason that the knocking sound echoed everywhere, especially if the street itself was narrow and delimited by tall buildings. Clappers or doorknockers were usually installed in pairs; the one mounted on the right-hand door panel (the part of a double door opened first) was used as the "bell", while the other clapper on the left was fixed and played a purely decorative role. The styling largely reflected the wall rings used to tie up horses, or to hold torches and flags. In the past, such extensive use ensured their huge popularity and craftsmen competed with each other to develop new styles.

Subjects were different in different places: in Malta, for example, dolphins were extremely popular, in a stylised, heraldic form with a sinuous body and the trident-shaped tail; they can still be seem on the main doors of buildings in the West End of London, brought home by Navy officers after service in the Mediterranean. They were sometimes made using moulds but were always finished by hand and quality is as varied as the figurative styles.

In truth, ring- or palm-shaped clappers were already common in classical Antiquity. In Greece and the territories incorporated in the Roman Empire, many base-plates have been found with hoops or rings joined to masques resembling lions, the Medusa and other mythological figures.

The initial classical experiences in the Humanist age were taken up and extended by skilful artisans who processed, engraved and hammered iron and bronze. In Italy, these craftsmen were generally active in Padua, Venice and Florence. Spain was still largely under Arab influence, while France and Germany were characterised by late-Gothic styles.

The simple ring thus developed into a variety of shapes (hearts, lyres, snakes) and was decorated with diamond-shaped tips, shells and medallions. Part of their success lay in the fact that as well as acting as knockers, they were also useful handles for opening and closing

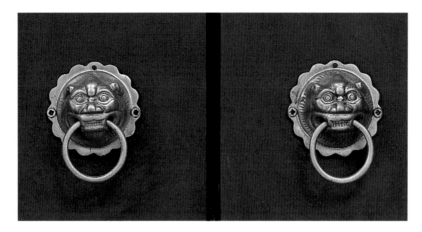

A vaguely neo-Gothic door-knocker in wrought iron.

Two door-knockers with animal figures in the centre of Singapore.

Again in Singapore, these bells serve to announce visitors, decorate the door itself and, above all, give the door important status.

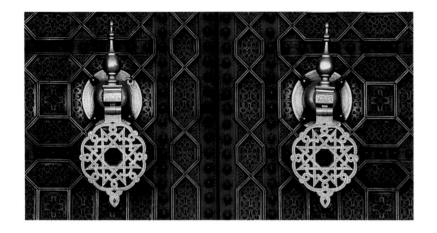

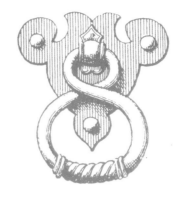

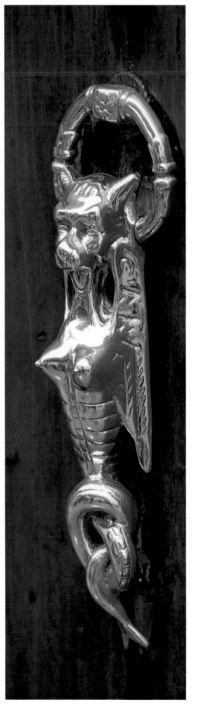

doors.

Placed in the centre of the door, the knocker was the main decorative element, though it also performed two important practical functions. Artists were stimulated by the need to "represent" their patrons and exploited these simple objects, turning them into important artefacts expressing complex symbolism.

During the Renaissance, many noble families commissioned door knockers with their own family shields, while other appeared with new figurative elements such as fauns, satyrs, dragons, sea gods and anything the fervid Humanist imagination was able to conjure up.

Unlike many other villa hallmarks, this detail did not originate from religious architecture, in the sense that knockers did not have to be screened, experimented with and approved by the architects of churches and monasteries.

Top left: curious brass clappers in Rabat, which have very limited movement.

Two overlapping S-shapes anchored to a triangular base-plate in this wrought iron knocker.

Left; two vertical clappers in polished brass. The dolphin comes from the island of Malta and the demonic figure from a door in Lima.

Side: a ring, polished by long use, serves as a doorknocker in Shanghai.

Side: two Florentine wrought iron doorknockers.

Below, left: the entrance to Sai Kung Village, Hong Kong, the mansion of a large and wealthy family.

Right: a simple iron knocker is hinged on a heavy wooden base (Sana'a, Yemen).

These buildings did not need devices to announce visitors: they were either open to all the faithful or closed to the laity. Knocking to announce arrival was a more typical requirement of private residences. Today, the role of clappers and knockers is performed by electric bells with pleasant ringing tunes or convenient video entry-phones. Other systems of announcement, not infrequently included in imaginative architectural settings, have now become merely decorative elements. Their survival, despite losing all trace of their original purpose, still bears witness to a time when the rhythms of life were slower and, perhaps, more human, when personal visits were not hurried affairs but enjoyed and savoured – right from the first insistent knocks of the clapper on the solid wood of the main door.

Star-shaped base plates are very common, especially in Neo-Gothic examples.

Even the doors to more modest Cypriot homes are graced by wrought iron knockers.

These two carefully polished rings adorn a door of the Sultan's Palace in Yogyakarta, Java, acting not only as knockers but also as handles.

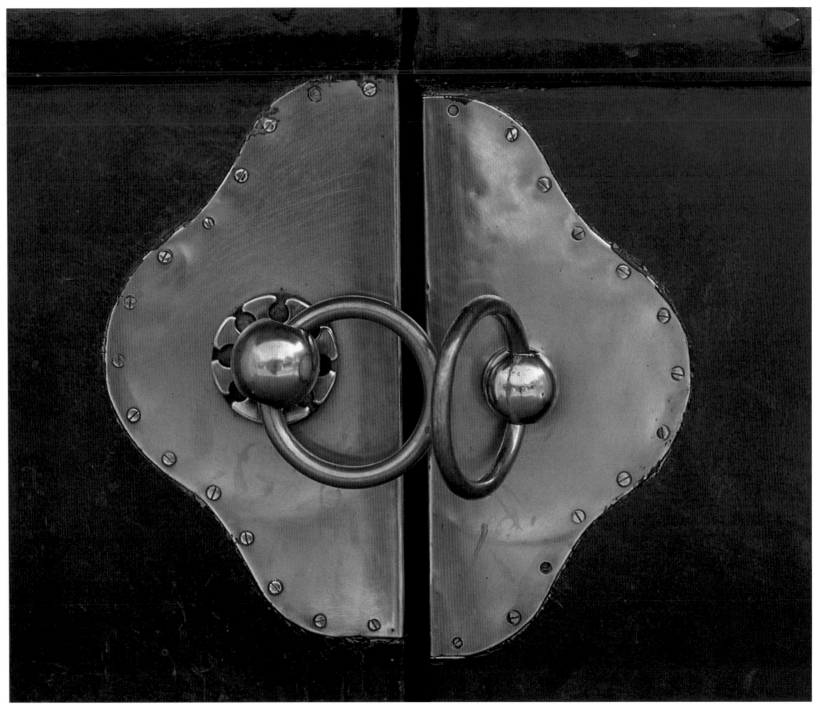

VILLA DETAILS

1

5

2

4

3

23

24

25

26

27

6

10

9

7 28 29 30 31 8 32

Gates

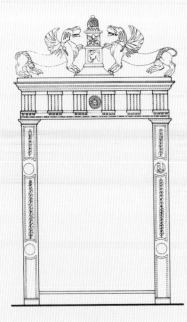

In every historical age or artistic season, the gates to houses, palaces and villas have responded to the need to emphasise - through suitable decoration - the prestige of their owners. Such embellishment included busts, shields, epigraphs and, indeed, anything and everything else in keeping with this intention.

In the paleo-Christian age and High Middle Ages, gates were rather austere; courtly residential architecture experienced a decline, since security was increasingly vital and visitors were welcomed to the chambers of noble families through castle gates, often after having first crossed a drawbridge. Only in religious buildings were doors more gracious and decorative

From the XII and XIII centuries, northern and central Italy saw the development of gates in a vaguely Classical style, often surmounted by skylights and decorated with bas-reliefs on the faces. The architecture of Emperor Frederick resumed the classical layout of gates, flanked by parastas and crowned by trabeations with a triangular load-bearing fronton. In the north of Italy, this feature was replaced by an arch performing the same function. At the same time, gates were embellished with concentric arches supported by pillars or columns.

In France, as the Gothic style became more and more popular, concentric arches were increasingly frequent in cathedrals and castles. At times, the aperture of the gate was widened and even divided in two by a central pillar, in turn often decorated with bas-reliefs. The Gothic period also saw the modification of these concentric gate arches into pointed arches. The late-Gothic age saw the spread of the so-called "Durazzo" gate in Catalonia and southern Italy, where the arch is lowered and set into a face, in turn marked off by more or less elaborate moulding. Renaissance gates were inspired by Roman models, although several variants were also introduced regarding not only proportions but also the composition of morphological elements. The models involved architraves and arched vaults, while mouldings were initially almost obsequious copies of classical examples. However, from the XVI century, inventiveness came increasingly to the fore, so much so that the Humanist period witnessed full-scale formal redevelopment. The so-called "aedicule" gate became extremely popular in this period; the

Above: the eclectic cornice of a main gate in Sestri Levante (Genoa). The main decorative motifs are inspired by Middle East art.

Following page: the main gate to the courtyard of Eggenberg, Graz, eastern Austria.

18

22

21

461

39

40

19

41

20

42

43

44

17

16

34

13

35

36

14

37

15

38

opening was based on the architrave or arched vault set into columns or parastas supporting both the horizontal trabeation and the triangular or semi-circular tympanum. This kind of gateway was exploited by a great many designers, including Antonio da Sangallo, Raphael, Michelangelo and Palladio. The "rustic" gate was characterised by the use of rough or smooth blocks of stone. Compositions were further embellished in the Mannerist period with the inclusion of such ashlars even in the orders, doubling up the load-bearing elements and, in particular, multiplying the number of mouldings, resulting in numerous personal variants by individual designers. Michelangelo was one of the supreme interpreters of this new design freedom; his many inventions include gates crowned by balconies with balusters. This was not an entirely new combination, although Michelangelo superbly blended the two elements into an architectural unity which dominated the whole facade.

In Spain and the Spanish colonies in the Americas, Baroque styles were embellished by exceptional decorative flourish, especially in the works of the churrigueresque architects, a trend which found minor echoes even in southern Italy. Following the excesses of Mannerism and the Baroque, the XVIII century in France and, especially, England saw a return to the pure and simple forms of the Classic age. Creativity and its exaggerations were abandoned, as well as formal experiments, to return to ancient rigour and simplicity. In the following century and through to our own times, developments went even further with the rediscovery of the various styles as evolved over the centuries, from the Romanesque to the Gothic and the Renaissance, including those not associated with classic tradition and thus embracing forms inspired by Egyptian, Oriental, Chinese and Japanese art.

The blending of so many different influences did not bring about a new style but encouraged a taste rightfully defined as eclectic.

Portals

The modern usage of the term "portal" indicates a monumental entrance to a building complex and may indicate both the main door to the residence as such and, more frequently, the entrance to its annexes, such as gardens, courtyards and the like. The portal links the public road with the architectural complex of the residence or other building, at times often used for new purposes. Portals are distinguished from doors and gates in hierarchical terms. They are more courtly, more important entrances characterised by impressive architectural and decorative status. Where doors and gates are unable to distinguish an entrance with due elegance, portals are installed. As already suggested, there are no specific features which identify and distinguish compositional nature so that it can be defined in absolute terms in

Shanghai: access to the Liu Gardens is through a circular doorway framed with black stone.

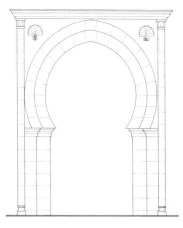

Two portals in sequence lead visitors into the Parisio Gardens of Naxxar, Malta.

Side: a portal with an ogival arch in Jerusalem.

Below: once sumptuous, this portal leads into one of the most important "caravanserai" on the ancient caravan route between Shiraz and Isfahan in Iran.

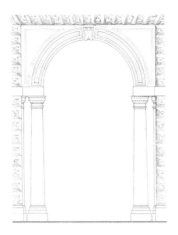

Opposite page, bottom right: stucco and plasterwork combine in this portal in Trujillo, Peru; emphasis is achieved through simple two-colour design.

Framed by rough ashlars, this portal graces one of the side walls of the Pitti Palace in Florence.

Light and shade emphasise a passageway between two courtyards in Rabat, one of the ancient imperial cities of Morocco.

Below: as courtly as it is false. A hint of skilfully reviewed classicism in tropical Honolulu merely provides access to a large courtyard.

one manner or another. There are too many different factors, not the least position, context (even environmental), materials, dimensions and, naturally, design.

All cultures, wherever possible, have always placed the main entrance in the centre of the facade. This dominant position itself emphasises the importance of entrances. However, a central position is not always possible, either because of pre-existing structures or other functional requirements. In such cases, the most common solution is to place the entrance on one side of the facade, preferably with a similar structure (true or dummy) on the opposite wing in order to restore symmetry. Theorising solutions and defining rules for the correct practice of architecture have been prevailing activities since Classical times, although the only example handed down to posterity is the treatise by Vitruvius, *De architectura*. The Roman essayist of the I century B.C. described doors as tapering slightly upwards, a design which was not particularly successful in later periods but which nevertheless took the name "Vitruvian". In any case, this treatise – rediscovered in the Renaissance – became a fundamental model for all later essayists, first of whom Leon Battista Alberti, whose *De re aedificatoria* published in 1425 suggests that portals should be "harmonised with the stature and frequency of men, and twice as high as wide". Sebastiano Serlio, in his *Sette libri dell'architettura* published in the mid-1500s, suggested thirty or so solutions for "rustic" entrances and around twenty for so-called "delicate" entrances. The latter include "Serlian" designs, doors (or

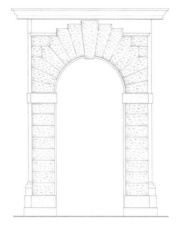

A triumph of Latin culture and tradition: this portal hides one of the most prestigious villas in Palm Beach.

Top right: the classic portal with rough ashlars from the Zanchini Corbinelli Palace in Florence.

Side: an ogival arch and merlons emphasise the entrance to Bait Na'Man, Oman.

windows) with three apertures: the larger, central opening is vaulted while the smaller side openings have trabeations. Vignola, in his treatise *Regola delli cinque ordini d'architettura* published in 1562, formulated two versions of Doric portals: one with motuli on the cornice, the other with dentils. Both styles may have triglyphs and be crowned by triangular or curved, continuous or interrupted frontons. Andrea Palladio in his *Quattro libri dell'architettura* (Fours Books on Architecture) printed in 1570, maintains that: "the architect, in designing main doors and gates, should accommodate the dimensions of the building, the importance of the owner and whatever has to pass through them". Moreover, the elements making up the portal may share the order used in the building itself, the order of the floor itself or neither of the two, thus creating a distinct contrast. Many contemporary designers took inspiration from these examples. Their interpretation of architectural elements became increasingly liberal: members were profiled, split and deformed in terms of ground plans and height to accentuate perspective. At times, canonical members were partly or entirely omitted to include new ornamental elements such as door-plates, coats of arms, scrolls, festoon and shells which were combined with considerable liberty in design style, which were difficult, if not impossible to trace back to definitive and repeatable outlines. Figurative elements became increasingly important: the masque-portal by Federico Zuccari in Rome is only one – albeit the most emblematic – of the many examples.

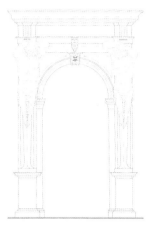

Top: two talamons support the cornice of this portal in the Durazzo Palace, Genoa.

Above: an arch-vaulted gate set beneath a triangular tympanum in Zanzibar.

Right: the enchanting gate to what could well be called the Disneyland of Coffee, in Merida, Venezuela, where there are many coffee plantations.

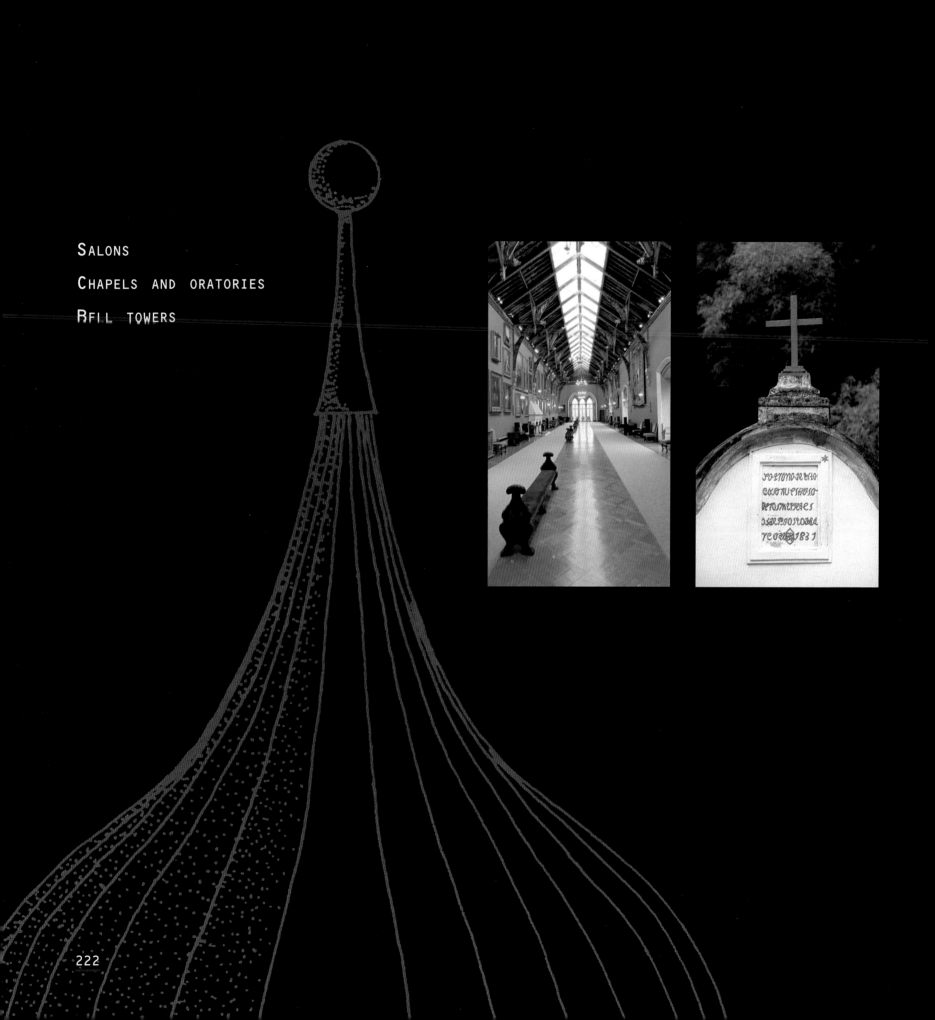

SALONS

CHAPELS AND ORATORIES

BELL TOWERS

The ballroom in Sinvbersvik Villa, Sweden, with an unusual parquet floor – held in high regard by pirouetting dancers during concerts.

The elliptical "eye" of the salon in Villa Strozzi in Bergozzo, the country home of the Strozzi nobles from Mantua.

The decoration of salons became increasingly eclectic in the 1800s.

The atrium-hall of Umaid Bawan Palace, the residence of the Sultan of Jodhpur, India.

A stucco shell in the main hall of Rivoli Castle, near Turin.

The trompe-l'oeil in one of the halls in the Pitti Palace, Florence.

Left: the pure white salon of Nottoway Hall, Louisiana, the mansion of an important cotton plantation owner.

Opposite page: mosaics, stuccowork, colour, carpets and precious fabrics enrich the salon of Dar Samai in Meknes, Morocco.

A stucco shell in the main hall of Rivoli Castle, near Turin, by Juvarra (XVIII century).

Superb trompe-l'oeil give depth to the walls of Villa Bozzolo at Casazuigno, near Varese, Italy.

The former courtyard of the Villa Patraia, Florence, was converted into a ballroom by King Vittorio Emanuele II.

French castles: they were rectangular, often decorated with works of art, stucco and paintings. Mirrors were later used to mitigate and vitalise these walls. The most famous Gallery of Mirrors is undoubtedly the 1600s "Galerie des Glaces", in the Palace of Versailles. Mirrors were later exploited in the Rococo period to provide an illusion of greater depth.

The prestige of a court was commensurate with the number of courtiers and servants, as well as the patronage of the arts evident in the main salon. The more artists the lord of the manor could afford, the more likely he was to be remembered. The emblem of his intellectual endeavours was the maze.

This was a symbolic image reproduced in gardens as well as in frescoes. It was a labyrinth of paths, all apparently identical, leading to the heart of the maze – an evident metaphor of intellectual life, always seeking truth which at times moves further away rather than coming within grasp. Salons, with one or two floors, accessible from the exterior or through a vestibule with or without tambours, took the place of the courtyards in Renaissance villas to ensure even greater courtliness.

Salons focused and amplified social rituals by celebrating the patron. Every culture and tradition has its equivalent: as time passed, relationships and importance may have changed, but salons and balls still retain their fascination.

Side: the "aquatic", open-air salon of Villa Portanuova, a 1960s villa overlooking the bay at Acapulco.

Above: a simple stucco moulding.

Below: long, narrow and somewhat Gothic, this salon is in Kilkenny Castle, Ireland.

Chapels and oratories

Two pillars topped by statues support the main gate opening on the Villa Bianchi in Mogliano, near Treviso, Italy.

Admirably blending the sacred and the profane, patrons and architects often devoted more energy to the art, ostentation, pride and self-celebration of these annexes than to the villa itself. Today, they are more than ever status symbols sought after by nobles and parvenu alike. The quasi holiness of Renaissance nobles transformed mansions into all-but sacred places. Nobles were not only responsible for managing large estates but also the souls of their subjects, or at least their spiritual well-being, and inasmuch often built small churches. This was, all told, a welcome task since it could easily be transformed into the exercise of power and, fortunately, good taste and culture. The selection of architects, artists and the themes for altarpieces and frescoes became a creative act of considerable importance which the aristocracy could claim entirely their own. In any case, the concept of the divine right of power exploited by the Western Roman Emperors was further developed in the Christian era in Byzantium to the extent of general and long-standing acceptance. This background enabled the aristocracy to hold sway over even the religious life of their subjects.

Just as kings and emperors reserved for their own purposes large portions of the public buildings that they had commissioned, the patrons of chapels and oratories set up women's galleries and boxes so that they could attend public religious functions without mixing with the common-folk. In fact, many of these small churches were open even to outsiders, since they were the focal point of community life in the small hamlet, castle or estate.

While many fortified mansions boasted their own small chapels in the mid-1500s, they were by no means common in villas. Palladio rarely considered them and it was only towards the end of the century that landowners realised the social power pertaining to such places of worship. After all, very few people were in a position to organise private religious functions, let alone welcome bishops or cardinals during the pastoral visits. This encouraged a flood of applications to consecrate a room in a villa or to build a place specifically designed for holding mass and burying the dead.

The custom of private chapels spread throughout Europe and into the intensely Catholic Spanish colonies and, to a lesser extent, Portuguese domains. There were very few such examples in other colonies; non-Christian areas did not envisage private places of worship

The Escudero Estate is located near Manila, in the Philippines. The chapel is far more monumental than the villa itself.

Partly abandoned but still highly remarkable, this church flanks the fortified mansion at Cardigliano di Sopra, near Lecce, Italy.

The tambour of the 1700s chapel at Villa Picchetta, Novara, Italy.

The dark wood of this simple chapel contrasts with the white door and window fittings (Budir, southern Iceland).

This chapel, in Ca' del Lago, Cerea, Verona, is characterised by tall, painted columns.

other than the tiny houses of spirits still common today close by villas and mansions in South East Asia. The latter are miniature houses, largely wooden, standing at ground level or on top of posts in positions chosen following complex astrological assessments. At times, these small temples are somewhat larger and may even be built in concrete, subsequently painted and decorated. It is by no means rare to find these altars, with sticks of incense burning amidst perfumed garlands of jasmine flowers. The spirits even appreciate gifts of food, otherwise they may torment local people ungenerous in their veneration. Modern and ancient beliefs blend in a tradition which knows no class boundaries and brings together mansions and hovels.

Over and above religions, cultures and artistic traditions, the need to bring the gods close to home is a recurrent desire. Places of worship thus provide protection against the divine, enhance social status and exhibit power. If the building also involves artistic matters, then it may also be an ideal opportunity to create something not only good but also beautiful. This aspect, as regards private places of worship, is really only characteristic of the western world.

Side: every family village on the island of Bali has its own temple, such as this one in Kerambitan.

Below: chapels were occasionally built inside the villa itself, as in this case in Herreria, Ecuador.

Top: a double staircase leads to the terrace of the chapel at Villa Allegri, Grezzana, near Verona, Italy.

Above: this chapel at the Villa Barbini in Asolo, near Treviso, closely resembles a parish church.

Chapels and oratories

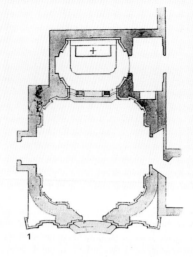

Despite their etymological differences, these two terms are by now virtually synonyms and used to indicate small, private or semi-private places of worship which may be independent or incorporated into a larger architectural complex, such as villas. The word "chapel" derives from the Latin "cappella", in turn the diminutive form of "cappa" (cloak), used with reference to the cloak of St. Martin of Tours, housed since the VII century in a small room in the Merovingian Royal Palace. Since this evolved into a place of veneration and prayer, the term came to be used to describe other places used for similar purposes.
On the other hand, the term "oratory" derives from the Latin "oratorium" or "orare" (to pray) and thus also indicates a place of worship, whether separate or inside the villa, used by a small and well-defined group of worshippers.
Both words thus describe a place set aside by a family (in a villa, for example) where, once it was consecrated by the appropriate Apostolic See, Mass could be celebrated.

Access is supervised and may be restricted to the private sphere (the owners of the villa), partly open to the public (guests are welcomed under certain conditions) or entirely public when all worshippers are welcomed. Chapels and oratories were already common in the early centuries of Christianity. They were generally small, rather isolated public places of prayer and usually had a very simple ground plan. The first such places reserved for specific worshippers were those built in the 1300s around the walls of Mediaeval castles, where the lord of the castle and his court or the small community of his subjects met to pray and worship. They began to assume precise architectural features from the 1400s, as well as greater importance – not the least in terms of decoration. Architecturally speaking, chapels and oratories generally had a single chamber, with vaults or exposed wooden frames. In some cases, there was a distinction between the nave and the presbytery, with an adjacent sacristy. There was usually only one altar located opposite the main

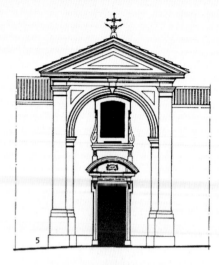

1. In the majority of Catholic chapels, the altar is separated from the main hall.

2. The chapel altar of the fortified Sciurlicchio estate in Puglia.

3. A simple altar enclosed by a vault.

4. A view of Montalto Pavese with the manor chapel in the foreground; painted by Giovanni Antonio Veneroni in 1735.

5. An impressive order framing the facade of this chapel in the Po Plains, Italy.

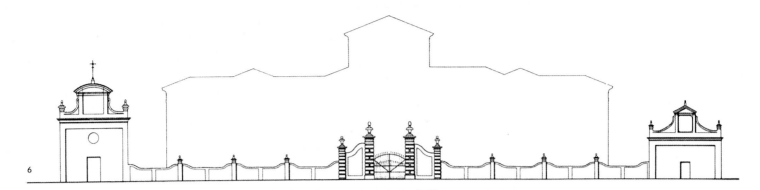

entrance, although there are also a few examples of such buildings with High Altars. Women's galleries were by no means rare. This kind of platform was placed above the main entrance or to the sides of the altar and could be accessed directly from the main building; the gallery was reserved for the manor family. There was often a wooden grating which hid the nobles from the view of their social inferiors.

Such chapels generally had a triangular or curved fronton, which hid the very simple roof. There were often two entrances: a private entrance from the villa itself and another entrance set in the main facade.

There were also simple bell-chambers in small towers or crowns.

Chapels and oratories were "noble" when essentially intended as places of worship or "funerary" when mainly intended as the last resting place of the lords of the manor.

6. The chapel of Villa Strozzi at Begozzo (Mantova) (left).

7. The cross-section of the temple designed by Palladio for the Villa Barbaro in Maser, Veneto.

8. The chapel of Villa Melin at Monselice, near Padua.

9. The curved facade of the chapel of the fortified estate at Cardigliano di Sopra, Puglia, Italy.

10. The main mansion and the chapel were often built side-by-side and communicated with each other.

11. Every fortified farmhouse in Puglia, southern Italy, had a chapel, often located to one side of the main facade.

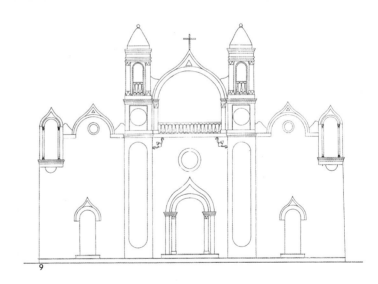

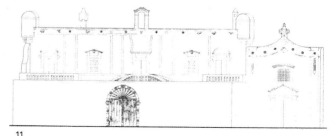

Bell towers

A double, crown bell tower at Hacienda Quimiapan, Jalara, Venezuela.

Mankind has always aspired skywards: physical height is linked with spirituality – God is on high and Paradise is inevitably in the Heavens. These beliefs are deep-rooted in every culture and religion, almost to the extent of belonging to the genetic code of all peoples. In ancient, pre-classical civilisations, temples stood on top of terraced pyramids. The base of the temple progressively descended earthwards, leaving adjacent towers the task of reaching for the sky: this, at least, was the case in both Western and Islamic culture.

Although building materials were very simple – bricks, stone and wood – the temptation of height was always immensely strong. The thick walls of early buildings became gradually lighter, giving rise to a structural framework within which architects soon learnt the impressive strength of stone. Early Christian churches and monasteries had towers, which also housed bell chambers.

In India, Indo-China and Indonesia, religious buildings are always characterised by vertical elements, although their impact is visual rather than audible. Even pagoda-style Buddhist temples – tall and narrow – are sacred towers built to be seen, not to be heard. Height also meets a specific acoustic requirement, since the higher the tower the better the proclamation of sound, be it the chant of the muezzin or the ringing of bells. This is why the bell chamber is always at the top of a tower. It is possible to climb some of these towers, others are exclusively used to house the bells and often have only steep metal ladders as a means of access.

Villa bell towers are smaller and more in keeping with courtly intentions. They are often simple wooden structures supporting the bell; in other cases, they are crowns set into a "fastigium" with an open space housing the bell itself. In dominical mansions, they not only call the faithful to religious functions but are also rung to mark the various times of day, such as noon or Ave Maria in the evening, as well as to sound an alarm in the event of danger. In the majority of cases, they are on the top or at the side of the chapel itself, although acoustic requirements may see them moved to the roof of the main building. At times, they are even quite separate from both buildings and supported by independent structures with arches or architraves.

Top: uncomplicated Spanish colonial architecture in Merida, Venezuela.

Above: a bell-tower combines with a belvedere in Selmunt Palace, Malta.

A simple crown bell tower over the chapel of Hacienda Cienega, Ecuador.

The pure white structure of this bell tower contrasts sharply with the deep blue of high-altitude sky at Hacienda La Comañia in Ecuador.

BIBLIOGRAPHY AND REFERENCES

There are few if any books devoted to the specific topic of "villa details". The majority of publications deal with architectural orders. The following references indicate a selection of specific books, encyclopaedias and dictionaries discussing these hallmarks and more general themes related to villas. They are arranged by geographical area and are by choice usually well-illustrated publications. This should enable readers to explore "villa details" on a regional basis.

ARCHITECTURAL ORDERS AND OTHER DETAILS

R. Adam, *Manuale di architettura classica*, Carnago, Sugarco, 1994.
P. Asti, *Una finestra sul tetto*, Milan, BE-MA, 1996.
F. Carria, *Ferro battuto in facciata. Tecniche, recupero, stili*, Milan, BE-MA, 1995.
R. Chitham, *Gli ordini classici in architettura*, Milan, Hoepli, 1987.
C. M. Cipolla, *Le macchine del tempo*, Bologna, Il Mulino, 1996.
G. Cusano, *La finestra e la comunicazione architettonica*, Bari, Dedalo, 1979.
L'escalier dans l'architecture de la Renaissance, Paris, Picard, 1985.
E. Heinle, *Torri. Architettura e storia dalla Torre di Babele al Word Trade Center di New York*, Milan, Mondadori, 1990.
G. M. Jonghi Lavarini – F. Magnani, *Sette secoli di ferro*, Milan, Di Bajo, 1991.
A. Lauria, *I balconi. Linee guida per la progettazione*, Rimini, Maggioli, 1998.
W. Lauter, *Porte e portoni dall'interno e dall'esterno*, Legnano, Edicart, 1989.
Il mondo delle torri. Da Babilonia a Manhattan, Milan, Mazzotta, 1990.
R. Morchio, *Scienza e poesia delle meridiane: piccolo manuale per leggerle e costruirle*, Genoa, ECIG, 1988.
G. Morolli, *"Le membra degli ornamenti". Sussidiario illustrato degli ordini architettonici con un glossario dei principali termini classici e classicistici*, Florence, Alinea, 1986.
G. Nones, *Al sol misuro i passi. Arte e tecnica dell'orologio solare*, Trento, Arca, 1994.
J. Onians, *Bearers of Meaning: the Classical Orders in Antiquity, the Middle Ages and the Renaissance*, Cambridge, Cambridge University Press, 1988.
G. C. Rigassio, *Le ore e le ombre: meridiane e orologi solari*, Milan, Mursia, 1988.
G. Rocco, *Introduzione allo studio degli ordini architettonici antichi*, Rome, Dedalo, 1995.
R. Rohr, *Meridiane: storia, teoria, pratica*, Turin, Ulisse, 1988.
F. Rossi, *La pittura di pietra*, Florence, Giunti, 1984.
B. E. Smith, *The Dome. A Study in the History of Ideas*, Princeton, Princeton University Press, 1978.
Lo specchio del cielo. Forme significati tecniche e funzioni dalla cupola dal Pantheon al Novecento, Milan, Electa, 1997.
Lo stucco da Bisanzio a Roma barocca, Venezia, Il Cardo, 1996.
Le superfici dell'architettura. Il cotto, Padua, Libreria Progetto, 1992.
Windows & Skylights, Menlo Park, Sunset Publishing, 1996.

ENCYCLOPAEDIAS AND DICTIONARIES OF ARCHITECTURE

Enciclopedia dell'architettura, Milan, Garzanti, 1996.
W. Koch, *Dizionario degli stili architettonici*, Varese, Sugarco, 1985.
Il nomenclator di architettura, Turin, Rosenberg & Sellier, 1993.
N. Pevsner - J. Fleming - H. Honour, *Dizionario di architettura*, Turin, Einaudi, 1992.
P. Portoghesi (a cura di), *Dizionario enciclopedico di architettura e urbanistica*, Rome 1968-1969.
A. C. Quatremere de Quincy, *Dizionario storico di architettura*, Venice, Marsilio, 1985.

VILLAS
America

F. Gagnon Pratte, *Maisons de campagne des montréalais 1892-1924*, Montréal, Éditions du Méridien, 1987.
H. M. Scott Smith, *The Historic Houses of Prince Edward Island*, Erin (Ontario), The Boston Mills Press, 1990.
A. Penney, *Houses of Nova Scotia*, Halifax (Nova Scotia, Canada), Formac Publishing Company, 1989.
A. Spoule - M. Pollard, *The Country House Guide*, Boston, Salem House Publishers, s.d.
M. Folsom, *Great American Mansions and Their Stories*, Mamaroneck (New York), Hastings House, 1963.
R. Schezen - J. Mulvagh - M. A. Weber, *Newport Houses*, New York, Rizzoli International Publications, 1989.

M. Randall, *The Mansions of Long Island's Gold Coast*, New York, Rizzoli International Publications, 1987.
D. K. Gleason, *Virginia Plantation Homes*, Baton Rouge and London, Louisiana State University Press, 1989.
B. Vila, *Guide to Historic Homes of the South*, New York, Lintel Press - Quill William Morrow, 1993.
J. Wesley Cooper, *Ante-Bellum Houses of Natchez*, Natchez (Mississippi), Southern Historical Publications, 1983.
C. J. Laughlin, *Ghosts Along the Mississippi*, New York, American Legacy Press, 1961.
M. Lane, *Architecture of the Old South. Mississippi & Alabama*, New York, Abbeville Press, 1989.
D. K. Gleason, *Plantation Homes of Louisiana and the Natchez Area*, Baton Rouge and London, Louisiana State University Press, 1982.
J. Arrigo - D. Dietrich, *Louisiana's Plantation Homes. The Grace and Grandeur*, Stillwater (Minnesota), Voyageur Press, 1991.
C. J. Laughlin, *The Magic of the Old Houses of Louisiana*, New York, American Legacy Press, 1987.
R. Schezen - S. Johnston, *Palm Beach Houses*, New York, Rizzoli International Publications, 1991.
P. Malone - L. Malone, *Louisiana Plantation Homes. A Return to Splendor*, Gretna (Louisiana), Pelican Publishing Company, 1992.
I. Macdonald-Smith - S. Shorto, *Bermuda Gardens & Houses*, New York, Rizzoli, 1996.
T. Street-Porter, *Casa Mexicana*, New York, Stewart Tabory & Chang, 1989.
M. E. García Ugarte - J. M. Rivero Torres, *Esplendor y poderío de las haciendas queretanas*, Queretaro (Mexico), Dirección de Patrimonio Cultural, Secretaría de Cultura y Bienestar Social, 1991.
R. Rendón Garcini, *Haciendas de México*, México D.F., Fomento cultural Banamex, 1994.
Caribbean Style, New York, Clarkson N. Potter, 1985.
J. Rigan, *Puerto Rico 1900. Turn-of-the-Century Architecture in the Hispanic Caribbean 1890-1930*, New York, Rizzoli International Publications, 1990.
Casa colombiana, Bogotà, Villegas, 1992.
B. Barney - F. Ramirez, *La arquitectura de las casas de hacienda en la Valle del Alto Cauca*, Bogotá, El Áncora, 1994.
G. Tellez, *Casa colonial. Arquitectura doméstica neogranadina*, Bogotá, Villegas, 1995.
Fazendas. Solares da Região Cafeeira do Brasil Imperial, Rio de Janeiro, Editora Nova Fronteira, 1990.
F. Tasso Fragoso Pires, *Fazendas. The Great Houses and Plantations of Brazil*, New York, Abbeville Press, 1995.
M. Sáenz Quesado - X. A. Verstraeten, *Estancias. The Great Houses and Ranches of Argentina*, New York, Abbeville Press, 1992.

Europe

J. O'Brien - D. Guinness, *Great Irish Houses and Castles*, London, George Weidenfeld & Nicolson, 1992.
Châteaux en Angleterre, Paris, Arthaud, 1989 (1st edition London, Viking, 1989).
The Country Life Book of Castles and Houses in Britain, London, Country Life Books, 1988.
F. J. Maroon, *The English Country House. A Tapestry of Ages*, Charlottesville (Virginia), Thomasson - Grant, 1987.
M. Di Niscemi, *Manor Houses and Castles of Sweden*, New York, Scala Books, 1988.
J. Ortmann, *Slotte og Herregårde i Danmark*, Viborg (Danmark), Sesam, 1994.
J. Guillermo - N. Sapieha, *Dutch Houses and Castles*, London, Tauris Parke Books, 1990.
Castella. Guide universel des châteaux du Benelux, Lierneux (Belgique), Eccho, 1992.
H. M. J. Tromp, *Kijk op Kastelen*, Amsterdam Bruxelles, Elsevier, 1980.
Guide des châteaux de Belgique, Bruxelles, Association Royal des Demeures Historiques de Belgique, 1992.
R. Schezen - L. Murat, *Francia meravigliosa. Palazzi, castelli, ville*, Milan, Rizzoli, 1991.
S. Chirol - P. Seydoux, *La Normandie des châteaux et des manoirs*, Paris, Chêne, 1989.
J. Dethier, *I castelli del Bordeaux*, Milano - Florence, Trainer International Editore - I libri del Bargello, 1991 (1ª ed. Paris, Editions du Centre Georges Pompidou, 1988).
O. Guaita, *Ville e giardini storici in Italia*, Milan, Electa, 1995.
R. Schezen - J. Basehart, *Italia meravigliosa. Palazzi, castelli, ville*, Milan, Rizzoli, 1990.
C. Roggero Bardelli - M. G. Vinardi - V. Defabiani, *Ville sabaude*, Milan, Rusconi, 1990.
P. F. Bagatti Valsecchi - A. M. CitoFilomarino - F. Süss, *Ville della Brianza*, Milan, Rusconi, 1980.

M. Matteucci - C. E. Manfredi - A. Còccioli Mastroviti, *Ville piacentine*, Piacenza, Tep, 1991.
R. Cevese, *Ville della provincia di Vicenza*, Milan, Rusconi, 1980.
E. Bassi, *Ville della provincia di Venezia*, Milan, Rusconi, 1987.
L. Zangheri, *Ville della provincia di Firenze. La città*, Milan, Rusconi, 1988.
N. Andreini Galli, *Ville pistoiesi*, Pistoia, Cassa di Risparmio di Pistoia e Pescia, 1989.
I. Belli Barsali, *Ville di Roma*, Milan, Rusconi, 1983.
I. Belli Barsali - M. G. Branchetti, *Ville della campagna romana*, Milan, Rusconi, 1981.
C. De Seta - L. Di Mauro - M. Perone, *Ville vesuviane*, Milan, Rusconi, 1980.
L. Mongiello, *Masserie di Puglia*, Bari, Mario Adda, 1989.
M. Pratt - G. Trumler, *Le grandi dimore dell'Europa Centrale. Ungheria, Cecoslovacchia, Polonia*, Udine, Magnus, 1991 (1st ed. New York, Abbeville Press, 1991).
Castelli d'Ungheria, s.l., Officina Nova, 1991.
F. Hauswirth, *Burghen führer der Schweitz*, s.l., Neptun Verlag Kreuzlingen, 1981.
C. Renfer - E. Widmer, *La Suisse des résidences. Châteaux, manoirs, maisons de maître*, Lausanne, Editions 24 heures, 1989.
M. Binney, *Casas nobres de Portugal*, Lisboa, Difel, 1987.
R. Dabo - J. Nuno Falcato, *Azulejos. Piastrelle decorative e architettura*, Milan, Silvana Editoriale, 1998.
R. Schezen - J. Junquera y Mato, *Spagna meravigliosa. Palazzi, castelli e ville*, Milan, Rizzoli, 1992.
O. Pi de Cabanyes, *Cases senyorials de Catalunya*, Barcelona, Edicion 62, 1990.
M. Caracciolo - F. Venturi, *Houses & Palaces of Majorca*, London, Tauris Parke Books, 1996.

Africa

N. Ghachem-Benkirane - R. Saharoff, *Marrakech. Demeures et jardins secrets*, Paris, ACR, 1990.
M. Eichler de Saint Jorre - N. Ardill - C. Bossu-Picat, *Demeures d'Archipel. Seychelles*, Mahé, Artistic Production, 1989.
C. Vaisse – C. Barat, *Cases créoles de la Réunion*, s.l., Les éditions du Pacifique, 1993.
C. Vaisse, *Maisons traditionnelles de l'île Maurice*, s.l., Albin Michel, 1990.
G. Viney, *Colonial Houses of South Africa*, Cape Town, Struik Winchester, 1988.
A. M. Obholzer - M. Baraitser - W. D. Malherbe, *The Cape House and its Interiors*, Stellenbosh (Cape Town), Stellenbosh Museum, 1985.

Asia

D. Kroyanker, *Gerusalemme l'architettura*, Venice, Arsenale Editrice, 1994.
S. Kay - D. Zandi, *Architectural Heritage of the Gulf*, Dubai, Motivate Publishing, 1991.
W. Dinteman, *Forts of Oman*, Dubai, Motivate Publishing, 1993.
G. Michel - A. Martinelli, *I palazzi reali dell'India*, Milan, Frassinelli, 1994.
R. Waterson, *The Living House. An Antropology of Architecture in South-East Asia*, Oxford, Oxford University Press, 1990.
T. Hock Beng, *Tropical Architecture and Interiors. Tradition-Based Design of Indonesia, Malaysia, Singapore, Thailand*, Singapore, Page One Publishing, 1994.
L. Invernizzi Tettoni - W. Warren, *Living in Thailand*, London, Thames and Hudson, 1988.
S. Naengnoi - M. Freeman, *Palaces of Bangkok. Royal Residences of the Chakri Dynasty*, London, Thames and Hudson, 1996.
T. Sosrowardoyo - P. Schoppert - S. Damais, *Java Style*, Singapore, Arcipelago Press, 1997.
K. Yeang, *The Architecture of Malaysia*, Amsterdam - Kuala Lumpur, The Pepin Press, 1992.
L. Invernizzi Tettoni, *Living in Sarawak*, London, Thames and Hudson, 1996.
Korean Ancient Palaces, Seoul, Youl Hwa Dang, 1988.
L. Invernizzi Tettoni - T. Sosrowardoyo, *Philipino Style*, London, Thames and Hudson, 1997.
R. Powell, *Tropical Asian House*, London, Thames and Hudson, 1996.

AUSTRALIA

The Historic Houses of Australia, Sydney, Australian National Trusts - Australian House & Garden Magazine, [1988].
T. Howells - M. Nicholson, *Towards the Dawn. Federation Architecture in Australia 1890-1915*, Sydney, Hale & Iremonger, 1989.

GLOSSARY

Abacus: Slab of stone placed on top of the capital; it has different designs depending on the order.

Acanthus: Wild plant common in the Mediterranean area, with large, frilly leaves; depicted in Corinthian capitals.

Acroterium: Decorative element placed at the summit or corners of a fronton. In some cases it indicates only the base supporting the decoration.

Aedicule: Small shrine suspended in a facade designed to host a statue.

Antefix: Vertical decoration once having a load-bearing function, located on the edge of the roof.

Antemium: Stylised vegetal motif.

Arabesque: Decoration with minute, stylised and repetitive geometrical or floral motifs introduced by the Arabs.

Architrave: The main beam of the trabeation, the upper element enclosing doors and windows.

Arms (coat of): Noble heraldic arms or patrician insignia shaped like a shield.

Ashlar: A squared-off block of stone, with more or less fine decoration.

Ashlared, bossed: Wall cladding with bosses and ashlars.

Atlas: Very large male figure supporting a trabeation in the place of a column or pillar.

Baluster: Small pillar or small column having a wide variety of shapes.

Balustrade: Baluster, series of balusters.

Belvedere: A raised place with views comprising architectural elements such as pavilions, terraces and turrets.

Boss: A squared-off block of stone.

Bucranium, Bucrane: Decorative motif in Classic art depicting the head of an ox between two festoons.

Capital: Decorated block of stone placed between the top of the column and the architrave/jamb.

Caisson: Lacunar decoration of a flat or curved ceiling.

Caryatid: Female figure taking the place of columns or pillars.

Chapsang: Small statue in vitreous clay placed on the roof of Chinese and Korean houses, depicting a warrior in a threatening pose considered to be the guardian of the home.

Cherub: Painted or sculpted portrayal of an angel in Christian religious art.

Corbel: Small arch supporting the shelves of merlons and embrasures.

Corbel: Overhanging load-bearing element.

Corbel plane: The load-bearing plane for arches and domes.

Cornice: Upper terminal band of a facade placed below the line of the gutters; also the decorative band outlining a doorway.

Cyma, cymatium: Framework crowning an architectural element.

Dado: Main component of the pedestal of a column.

Dentil: Tooth-shaped element in a cornice.

Dormer: Room set into the roof, which is illuminated by windows of various kinds.

Echinus: Overhanging element placed underneath the abacus of the capital of a column.

Embrasure: The gap between the corbels supporting merlons, used to drop objects on to besieging forces.

Entasis: The increase in the cross-section of the drums in a column.

Eye: Round or oval window especially used in the Baroque and Rococo styles.

Face: External emphasis of a room involving vertical and horizontal cornices.

Festoon: Bas-relief or painted decoration in the form of garlands of branches with flowers and putti suspended from the two ends.

Flat arch, piataband: Low arch used in place of an architrave to enclose the upper part of doors and small windows.

Frieze: Horizontal decorative band in the centre of the trabeation; various styles depending on the order.

Groove: Vertical concavity along the drums of a column.

Grotesque: Decoration inspired by arabesques with sphinxes, leaves, branches and animals, in fresco or stuccowork styles.

Grotto: Natural or artificial cave-like place, cool in hot summer months; also associated with a vague sense of mystery.

Guilloche: Decoration comprising interweaving ribbons used to embellish door and window frames.

Guttae, drops: Small, cylindrical decorative element originally used only in the Doric order.

Hermae: Support for architraves having human forms used for decorative and static purposes.

Hermitage: Isolated and solitary place generally characterised by a walled area used for meditation.

Impost: Block on which the arch stands, usually overhanging.

Lunette, fanlight: Kind of window above a door.

Merlon: Tooth-like (square or swallow-tail) crenellation (merlon) of perimeter walls in fortified buildings.

Metope: Space between two triglyphs in Doric friezes.

Modillion, truss: Small corbel in Corinthian or composite orders.

Motulus: Decorative element typical of Classic trabeations jutting out under the cornice.

Moulding: Continuous decorative element, smooth or with repeated motifs.

Oculus: Round opening in the centre of a dome.

Ovolo, echinus: Component of mouldings, convex, shaped like a halved egg.

Parastas: Pillar slightly jutting out from the row or wall, similar to a pilaster strip but having static functions.

Pebble: Round stone honed by water used to pave avenues in gardens and to decorate grottoes.

Pendentive: A curved triangle of vaulting formed by the intersection of a dome with its supporting arches.

Peristyle: A colonnade that surrounds a court or building, portico around a courtyard.

Pilaster strip: Relief on a wall, originally without a base or capital, having an essentially decorative function.

Propylaeum: Entrance to monumental buildings with several doorways.

Pulvinar: Convex, overhanging frieze used as decoration.

Putto: Statue depicting a young boy, generally nude, often used as a decorative element in fountains.

Quadrature: Architecture painted on walls applying the rules of perspective, fashionable in the 1600-1700s; undertaken by "quadraturists".

Ribbing: The line of intersection between two vaults.

Rocaille: Decoration comprising rocks, shells and stalactites especially employed in grottoes at the end of the 1500s. The term also indicates a period in the Rococo style.

Rosette: Round decorative element with a stylised flower in the centre.

Scroll ornament, cartouche: Decoration comprising a scrolled cornice with an inscription or coat of arms inside.

Serlian window: Window with a large central aperture, generally arched, and two smaller sides often surmounted by an eye. Designed for the first time by Serlio, it was extensively used by Palladio.

Skylight: Element crowning a roof or dome, generally in the form of a circular or polygonal turret, used to provide light to the areas below.

Span: The distance between the centre-line of two columns in a colonnade.

Sponge: Artificial cladding reproducing rock walls, stalactites and stalagmites, used in grottoes.

Storey-marker: Decorative horizontal band placed on the facade at the ceiling/floor between two storeys.

Tambour: Cylinder linking a dome and the load-bearing masonry, generally used in roofing salons and chapels.

Telamon: Pillar resembling a male figure.
Torus: Convex moulding at the base of a column.

Trabeation: Element comprising the architrave, frieze and cornice, supported by columns in Classic orders.

Triglyph: Part of a frieze in the Doric order, alternating with the metope.

Trompe-l'oeil: From the French, meaning "trick of the eye", wall painting simulating architecture or landscapes to expand space through illusion.

Urn: Ancient vase used for cremation ashes included in Romantic parks as archaeological relics.

Veil: Each of the parts into which a vault is divided.

Vestibule: Antechamber or entrance to salons.

Volute: Compositional element characterised by spiral lines.